CLASS DEVOTIONS

CLASS DEVOTIONS
for use with the
1979-80 International
Lessons

HAROLD L. FAIR

ABINGDON
Nashville

CLASS DEVOTIONS
for use with the 1979-80 International Lessons

Copyright © 1979 by Abingdon

ISBN 0-687-08619-1

Scripture quotations unless otherwise noted are from
the Revised Standard Version of the Bible, copyrighted
1946, 1952, © 1971, 1973 by the Division of Christian
Education of the National Council of Churches of Christ
in the U.S.A.

MANUFACTURED BY THE PARTHENON PRESS AT
NASHVILLE, TENNESSEE, UNITED STATES OF AMERICA

To my brother
Jim
and my sister
Shirley

adversaries as children
friends as adults

Preface

"How will this book help me?" The question comes to men, women, and young people who are asked to present the devotional at the next meeting of their group.

What is the purpose of a devotional? It is a transition time when members of the group are called to move from the secular realm to the spiritual realm. It serves as the buffer zone where we are called to think about our responsibilities as we stand before God. It reminds us that we are moving into the life of the spirit.

Each devotional in this book has a suggested scripture reading, a brief message, and a prayer. The scripture passage should always be read aloud. You may wish to use a modern translation. The message in each devotional begins with a story or an account of some historical event and ends with an application of the scripture reading to our lives today. A short prayer concludes each devotional. You may wish to ask the group to sing a hymn before the closing prayer.

The devotionals in this book are related to Sunday school lessons, but they are also adaptable to the youth group, the women's meeting, or the men's club.

This book goes out with the hope and prayer that the messages here will assist men, women, and young people in their quest to find new life in Christ.

Contents

READ FROM YOUR BIBLE: GENESIS 1:1-13.

And It Was Good

On a morning in the year 1888, Alfred Nobel, the scientist who invented dynamite, saw an account of *his own* death in a daily newspaper. The newspaper had made an error; it was his brother who had died the day before.

As he read the account of his life and death, Nobel was shocked. The paper called him the "dynamite king" and referred to him as a merchant of destruction. When Nobel saw what the newspaper said about him, he was determined that he would find a way to make the true meaning of his life clear to the world.

Alfred Nobel was born in Sweden. Because he was a sickly child, he went to school only one year of his life, but was taught at home by his mother and special teachers. When he was a young man, he began to experiment with the explosive nitroglycerin. At that time, all explosives were dangerous, even to those who were experts in handling them. Accidents were not unusual. In 1866, a ship carrying a small amount of nitroglycerin blew up in a harbor on the coast of Panama. Thirty men were killed and many others seriously injured.

Nobel wanted to develop an explosive that could be used safely. After many experiments, he invented dynamite. This invention along with others that followed made him a wealthy man. The building of canals, mines, and other peaceful uses of dynamite were the goal of his work on explosives. His intention was to benefit humanity.

After the mistaken account of his death appeared in the newspapers, Nobel began to think more seriously about his life. Since he had never married, he had no immediate family who would inherit his wealth. He decided that he would leave his entire fortune in a fund that would give annual awards to those persons who had done the most to benefit humanity in chemistry, physics, medicine, literature, and peace.

11

Eight years after the erroneous account of his death appeared, Nobel died. The first prizes to carry his name were awarded five years later, in 1901. Since that time, many worthy people have received the recognition and honor of a Nobel prize.

Nobel's invention, dynamite, has been used to the great benefit of humanity. But it has also been used for destructive purposes. Persons have been murdered when dynamite was placed in their automobile. Dynamite has been used by thieves to blow up bank vaults and to open safes. It has been used by terrorists to destroy bridges and buildings and to maim and kill men, women, and children. Nobel intended his invention for good, but it has been used by evil people for selfish ends.

In the scripture reading we have heard today, the writer describes God's view of his creation. When he created light on the first day, he saw that it was good (verse 4). When he created the earth and the seas, he saw that they were good (verse 10). We have the clear impression when we read this account that God was pleased with his creation.

As we look at the world about us today, we thank God for the beauty of the earth, for the skies, for the day and night, for human love between brother, sister, parent, and child. On every hand, we see the results of the work of those who have tried to make the earth a more beautiful place to live. Like God, we see our world as a good creation.

Yet we also see the destruction humanity has brought to earth. Polluted land, water, and air are examples of what happens when people think only of themselves. We must think of the generations who will live after ours. Will they too see the beauty of the earth God made or will they see only the ruins of God's creation?

We are told that we are living at a critical time in the earth's history. Alfred Nobel was appalled when he read the mistaken account of his death which said that he would be remembered as a "merchant of destruction." Thereafter, he directed his life in a different way, and the prizes he established remain as his desire to benefit humanity.

As we live in God's world, let us remember that on the

sixth day he created male and female and to them—and to us—he has given all that he has created. Will future generations see our generation as merchants of destruction who destroyed the earth that God called "good"?

Let us pray:
O God, whose will is life and good, help us to be responsible stewards of the beautiful world you have made. May we live in such a way as to leave to coming generations a better world than we found. In the name of Christ. Amen.

READ FROM YOUR BIBLE: PSALM 106:1-12.

A People Who Forgot

The name of Patrick Henry is known to every child who has studied American history. The speech he made in 1775 that ended with the words, "Give me liberty, or give me death," made him one of the best-known patriots in the American colonies.

Patrick Henry was born not far from Richmond, Virginia, in the year 1736. As a young man, he did not care much for school, but preferred to spend his time with the woods and streams of his state. When he was only sixteen years old, he and his brother opened a country store, but their business failed. Two years later, he got married, though he had no regular income. His wife's parents set them up on a farm with a few slaves. When he was twenty, he opened another store, but again failed.

Patrick Henry was determined to make a success of himself, and when he was twenty-three years old, he began the study of law. In only a year, he learned enough to pass the examinations. Right away, he became a popular lawyer,

13

and though he had gotten a late start—at that time a man of twenty-four was considered middle aged—he handled over a thousand cases in the first three years of his practice.

Five years after he became a lawyer, he was elected to the Virginia legislature. When the Stamp Act, a new tax on the people of the American colonies, was passed in 1765, Patrick Henry's speeches resulted in Virginia's becoming the first state to make an official protest.

As he became more involved in state government, Henry became concerned about colonial rights. In 1775, he began to argue that the state should raise its own army. On March 23, 1775, at a patriotic convention that was meeting in St. John's Church in Richmond, Patrick Henry made his famous speech. He closed with these stirring words: "Why stand we here idle? What is it that gentlemen wish? What would they have? Is life so dear, or peace so sweet, as to be purchased at the price of chains and slavery? Forbid it, Almighty God! I know not what course others may take, but as for me, give me liberty, or give me death!"

In less than a month after this speech was made, the War of the Revolution began. It was fought by people who believed that their cause was right and who risked everything for freedom.

Today we sometimes forget the patriotism, courage, and honesty of those who fought to make this land free. Sometimes we are a people who have forgotten.

In the psalm we have heard today, the writer calls on the Hebrew people to remember what God has done for them. When their fathers were in Egypt, they did not consider the wonderful works of the Lord. Yet he saved them at the Red Sea. Psalm 106 recites other times when the people forgot the God who had saved them. In the wilderness, they criticized God. They made a golden calf and worshiped it. They did not believe God's promise that he would give them a pleasant land. Even after they inherited the Promised Land, they sacrificed to idols. Because the people forgot the God who had saved them, he gave them over to other nations. "Many times he delivered them, but they were rebellious in their purposes" (verse 43). When they cried out

14

in distress, he heard their cry. He remembered them. But they were a people who forgot.

Today, in this free land, we too forget the sacrifices of men like Patrick Henry who were willing to die in defense of liberty. Many people criticize our form of government. They criticize public officials who are doing the best they can to serve people. When men and women in politics do wrong, they should be criticized. But many people at every level of government are sincerely trying to make our system work. They need our help as responsible citizens. When we say, "Let others do it," we are a people who have forgotten the patriots who founded our nation.

As Christians too, we often forget. We forget the God who made and rules the earth, who gave us life, and who gave us his son as our savior. Since we claim to worship God, let us not be a people who forgets.

Let us pray:

O God, beneath your guiding hand, our forefathers and mothers came to this land. Permit us not to forget the sacrifices they made for us. But most of all, let us not forget you, who have given us all we possess, and especially Jesus Christ, in whose name we pray. Amen.

SEPTEMBER 16, 1979
READ FROM YOUR BIBLE: MATTHEW 13:24-30.

A Church Without Sinners?

The first humans who lived on the earth found their food by hunting, fishing, and searching for wild plants. Thousands of years later, they discovered that seeds could be planted and food could be grown. They also discovered that animals could be tamed and made to work. More than five thousand years ago, the ox-drawn plow was invented. After the plow came into use, farmers were able to grow more food than they needed to feed their families. As cities in the ancient world grew in number and size, the extra food grown by farmers was sold to markets in the cities.

In our time, many persons have developed a personal interest in farming. The increasing price of food in the stores has led many people to begin a small garden to grow vegetables. This same interest has led many others to go into the forests to seek plants that can be used for food. Finding plants in the forest that are fit for human consumption can be a problem, however. Many plants that look good enough to eat are actually poisonous.

A person might mistake the deadly toadstool for mushrooms. One kind of toadstool is so poisonous that it is called the "destroying angel." Of those who eat it, more than half may die or suffer permanent liver damage. The careless person might mistake water hemlock for wild parsnips. Only a few bites of hemlock are enough to kill an adult. In the woods there grows a plant with fruit that looks like grapes; yet this plant is actually the poisonous moonseed. Birds may eat it and not be harmed, but it can be fatal to humans.

Although many tasty foods can be found in the woods, only the person who knows the difference between what is poisonous and what is not should gather and eat these plants and fruits.

In our scripture reading for today, Jesus told the parable of the weeds sown among the wheat. When the servants asked if they should go into the fields and pull the weeds, the owner told them to let both grow together until the time of harvest. Then the weeds would be gathered and burned and the wheat would be placed in the barn.

What point was Jesus making in this parable? The idea he was probably trying to get over was that even among his followers there would be some who would be harmful or bear no fruit. In the early days of the church, many people thought the church should be perfectly pure. No sinners should be allowed.

16

As time went on, people began to see that "all have sinned and fall short of the glory of God" (Romans 3:23). Sin is any act that violates God's moral law. For an act to be sinful, an evil motive is required. This evil motive may be our own pride or selfishness. When we think about accusing others, we must consider their motives. But since we are human and cannot know the hearts of others, we cannot judge them. Only God can do that.

Since we are all sinners, according to the scriptures and our own self-knowledge, the church can never be totally pure. Only Jesus Christ lived a sinless life. Therefore, sinners will always be a part of the church.

This parable teaches us, therefore, that only God can judge. Because we are human, we may make mistakes in judgment. Like an untrained person who goes into the woods to look for food and passes over plants that are good to eat because they look like plants that are poisonous, we may make mistakes and judge others wrongly.

Let us live a life of love and openness, therefore, and let God be the judge. We too are sinners. Only in heaven can there be a church without sinners.

Let us pray:

O God of love, forgive us when we try to take your place in judging others. Even as we pray that you will forgive our faults and errors, may we also be charitable toward the faults and errors we think we see in other people. In the name of Christ. Amen.

SEPTEMBER 23, 1979
READ FROM YOUR BIBLE: I TIMOTHY 4:6-16.

Setting Our Hope on God

Charles enlisted in the Marine Corps in 1965 and soon found himself in Vietnam. Although he had been raised in the church, he had not made it an active part of his life for a long time.

Something happened to him during the war that changed his life. One night he went to see the motion picture, *The Ten Commandments,* and, for the first time in many years, he began to think seriously about his faith.

A few months later, he had another experience that seemed to confirm his religious feelings. It happened one evening when he was out walking. He was wearing a jacket that would protect him againt fragments of a mortar or hand grenade, but it was not buttoned. Then out of nowhere, it seemed, appeared a Marine lieutenant who yelled at him to button his jacket. Only a few minutes later as he was walking down a small but steep hill, he stumbled and fell, rolling into a thick bush whose branches had been sharpened by the enemy to wound or kill any American who fell against it. The sharpened stake struck him in the chest right in the place where only moments before his jacket had been open. He was convinced that the officer's warning had come from God.

After his service in the Marine Corps was finished and the war was over, he returned to New York City. He went to church regularly because he was seeking God's guidance for his life. He didn't know what kind of job to look for. All he knew was that he wanted a place where he could serve God.

The job he finally got was taking care of the torch of the Statue of Liberty. He decided that the statue would become a chapel where he could worship God. Each day at work, he spent some time there in prayer. His witness became that of speaking to tourists about his faith whenever he had the opportunity and of handing out tracts to visitors if they showed an interest.

To many persons, his witness may seem small. But it is Charles' way of thanking God for saving his life in Vietnam. He has little education and few gifts, but he is using what he has to praise God and to show a good example.

In the scripture passage we have heard today, Paul urges Timothy to train himself in godliness. It is godliness, he says, that "holds promise for the present life and also for the life to come" (verse 8). We should strive to attain godliness, "because we have our hope set on the living God, who is the Savior of all men, especially of those who believe" (verse 10).

Young Timothy is also told that he should "set the believers an example in speech and conduct, in love, in faith, in purity" (verse 12). He should not neglect the gift he has received.

The young Vietnam veteran, Charles, and the young missionary, Timothy, tried to show the good example. Every Christian is obligated to witness through the good example of his or her life. Many persons do not have the gifts to be a preacher, teacher, doctor, or other public servant. But every one of us can take leadership by being a good example.

Paul writes in his letter that Timothy should train himself in godliness. This advice is good for us also. Training ourselves in godliness is of value because it prepares us both for this life and for the life to come. Training in godliness is not easy. It requires discipline and attention.

Next year the Olympics will be held. Today thousands of young men and women are in training for those games. They think of little else than the goal before them. They do nothing that might hinder their chances of winning. Proper food, rest, and exercise are part of their training. Out there in the future is the prospect of a gold medal. They make each sacrifice with that goal in mind.

Godliness is our goal. Like those in training for the Olympic games, we must make any sacrifice to achieve that goal. As we bend our minds and our energies toward the goal of godliness, we will become the good example. We must set our hope on God.

Let us pray:

Come, Holy Spirit, into our lives and anoint us with the power to be a good example. When you are our guide, we shall be kindled with that holy flame that leads to true godliness. Let us set our hope on God. We make this prayer in Jesus' name. Amen.

The Water of Life

On the afternoon of May 31, 1889, the people of Johnstown, Pennsylvania, were worried because of heavy rains. In one part of the city, water was already knee deep. A boy, whose father was concerned over the safety of a pair of horses in the stable, ran outside to lead them to the barn, which was on higher ground.

As the sixteen-year-old told the story later, he first heard a roar punctuated by several crashes. Looking back toward the house, he saw his father motioning for him to climb to the top of the barn. In a few moments he was high enough to see a wall of water coming toward him. He knew what had happened: the dam above the town had broken. The Johnstown flood of 1889 had begun.

The boy could see the wall of water moving his direction. It really didn't look like water, for it was a dark mass that contained houses, railroad cars, and trees. He looked at his watch. It was 4:20. The water got to the street below him, and as he watched from the top of the barn, the house where his father had stood only moments before was crushed and carried away. He never saw his mother or father alive again.

The big barn was pulled from its foundation, and the boy held to the roof as it was swept along in the flood. Everywhere about him he could hear the screams of the injured. He knew people were being killed. As the roof of the barn passed a two-story brick house on a hill near the town, he hopped to the roof of the house joining several other people who were stranded there.

He looked back toward town, and what he saw was a scene of almost total destruction. Again he looked at his watch. It showed 4:30. In only ten minutes, Johnstown, Pennsylvania, had been destroyed and three thousand lives had been lost.

In 1937, the Ohio River rose more than fifty feet above normal levels. More than nine hundred persons were killed, and almost one million people were driven from their homes. Property damage was estimated at more than four hundred million dollars.

Flood waters are often rivers of death. Contrast in your mind the waters of death with the reading we have heard today on the water of life. The writer of the book of Revelation had a vision of a new heaven and a new earth. He saw the holy city, the new Jerusalem, and he heard a voice saying that the dwelling of God is among his people. " 'He will dwell with them, and they shall be his people, and God himself will be with them; he will wipe away every tear from their eyes, and death shall be no more, neither shall there be mourning nor crying nor pain any more, for the former things have passed away' " (verse 4). Then God promised that to the thirsty he would " 'give water without price from the fountain of the water of life' " (verse 6).

Who shall have this heritage? According to this reading, the person who conquers. The heritage shall come to those who, by and through God's grace, are faithful to the end.

Life for many of us is filled with temptations. Sin slips upon us when we become proud and self-reliant. We must always be alert against the possibility that we shall come to feel that we do not need God's help in the war against sin. We may become self-righteous and hypocritical, feeling ourselves better than others. In those moments, we are in greatest danger.

We cannot win the battle against sin by our own power. We must turn to God in humility and pray daily for his help; we must be thirsty for him. Only in this way will we conquer and be children of God, invited to drink " 'without price from the fountain of the water of life.' "

Sin without forgiveness will bring the flood waters of death. Like the boy in the Johnstown flood, we must find a place where we will be safe from the waters of death. For the Christian, Christ is the rock—our protection. He is the one who can give us the water of life.

Let us pray:

Gracious Father, we know in this quiet moment that we have sinned and have fallen short of your glory. We cannot be perfect and sometimes we cannot even be good. We come to you in faith and ask for the water of eternal life. Through Christ, we pray. Amen.

OCTOBER 7, 1979

READ FROM YOUR BIBLE: LUKE 12:22-31.

Do Not Be Anxious

At six o'clock in the morning of June 24, 1948, the Soviet Union stopped all rail, highway, and water traffic into the city of Berlin. The city of more than two million West Germans could not survive without food and fuel from outside the city. The question arose of whether the Allies would stay in Berlin or would give it up to complete Soviet control.

General Lucius Clay, the American governor of Germany, stated that only war could drive out the Allies. But how would the people of the city be kept alive? With rail, highway, and river traffic stopped, the only possibility was by air.

The Berlin Airlift was born. At first, the problems seemed too great to be solved. President Truman ordered that every available American plane was to be pressed into service. Within a week, the planes were hauling nearly four hundred tons of supplies every twenty-four hours.

The people of Berlin had suffered greatly during the last weeks of the war. With peace came the black market. Butter cost sixty dollars a pound, and a pair of secondhand shoes could cost more than a hundred dollars. Now they knew they would suffer even greater hardships under the blockade.

The airlift got under way, and Allied air and ground crews showed heroic dedication to their task of bringing in

22

food. When a plane landed in West Berlin, an unloading crew came aboard. As the cargo was being removed, the plane was refueled. A snack bar on wheels brought food for the flight crew, who were required to stay near the plane.

By October of 1948, four months after the airlift began, planes were taking off at the rate of one every three minutes night and day. The people of West Berlin had less than half the amount of food coming in than they had had before. Everyone was worried about the coming of cold weather. Some people were starving, and children could not concentrate in school because they were so hungry.

As the winter became more severe, food deliveries were cut in order to bring in more coal. But the planes kept right on flying, and the people of West Berlin held out. Not until May 12, 1949, after nearly eleven months, did the Russians give in, when they saw they could not starve the German city into submission and drive out the Allies. The Berlin Airlift had become one of the finest hours of the free world.

What Jesus was saying in the passage we have heard is that we must live in the care of God. He does not say that we should have no concern whatever, but says that we are not to allow ourselves to become anxious or sick with worry about the future. We live in a world that is feverish with worry—but worry about material things. When Jesus said that we are not to be anxious, he did not mean that we should not pray and work. He was telling us that we should have courage, that we should accept each day as a gift from God, and that we should trust in him.

The situation of the Allies and the people of West Berlin illustrates the deeper meaning of Jesus' words. If they had been taken in the shallow sense, the people would have given in to the Russians and the Allies would have never attempted the airlift. But an effort was made. The men who loaded and flew the planes believed in their mission. Therefore, they were not uncertain or afraid. They were courageous and sure of the rightness of the task before them. The people of the city also believed they were right, and they were willing to undergo terrible sacrifices.

The word of Jesus to us today is to have courage, to trust

in God, to work and to pray. If we have this attitude, we won't be anxious about the future. We will know that our times are in God's hands.

Let us pray:

O God, before whose altar we bow in prayer, we thank you for your kind providence in all of life. May we always work and pray, and let us not become paralyzed with fear. We make our prayer as an expression of our faith in Christ. Amen.

OCTOBER 14, 1979

READ FROM YOUR BIBLE: MARK 10:35-45.

Being Great—Being a Servant

In 1967, a young man who had just completed college and graduate school volunteered for combat duty in Vietnam. He served eleven months, attained the rank of captain, and received both the Silver and Bronze stars.

Early in 1968, with only a month remaining before he would be taken out of combat, he was helping unload a helicopter. He saw a hand grenade on the ground, but before he could get to it, it exploded. As a result, the young soldier lost both legs and his right arm.

Although he was a hero, he was not sent home. Instead, he went to an army hospital where he seemed to become only a number among the thousands of men wounded in Vietnam. Months after the explosion on the battlefield, he experienced a terrible letdown. The excitement of battle and the support of his comrades was gone. He kept asking the question, "Why me?"

Following several months in the hospital, he returned to his home. When he thought about his future, he knew that he could live the remainder of his life in his home town on the pension he received. Soon he discarded that idea. As he searched his mind for a career, he decided to go into politics. He especially wanted to help the handicapped veterans of our nation's wars.

Only three years after he was wounded, he was elected to the senate of his state. He sponsored, and the legislature passed, a number of bills to help the handicapped. Then in 1977, he was selected to be the head of the Veterans Administration in Washington. His biggest objective was to help veterans return to work.

Here was a man who had served his nation in war and might have settled down to let others wait on him. He could have decided that there was little future for a man who had lost two legs and an arm, but he was determined to help others. Rather than being served, he wanted to serve.

Someone asked him why he did it. He replied that the grace of God made him sensitive to the needs of others. As long as we live on this earth, he said, we must be our brother's keeper.

In the scripture reading we have heard today, James and John asked Jesus for places of honor in his kingdom. When the other disciples heard of this selfish request, they were indignant. Jesus then called them together and told them that in the outside world great men lorded their authority over others. Among his followers, he said, whoever wished to be great would be the servant of all. He said that he himself came not to be served but to serve.

These words of Jesus are at the heart of his message. During all the years of his ministry, he had little comfort from material possessions. His ministry was active, and he went from place to place, teaching and healing. These works of love were soon forgotten when the crowds in Jerusalem cried out for his crucifixion.

Today Christians must examine their lives to see if they are guilty of the selfishness of James and John. Perhaps we too sometimes seek places of honor instead of places of service. Certainly we feel good if we are recognized with a position of importance, but it is more important to have the recognition of God than the recognition of other persons.

In every organization, in every community, God's work must be done by human hands. We may take the attitude that because of our age or importance we can let others wait on us. If we feel this way, we should remember the example of the Vietnam veteran who wanted to help others. We should also recall these words of Jesus so that they become our slogan in life. "Whoever would be great among you must be your servant, and whoever would be first among you must be the slave of all."

Let us pray:

O Thou who came from above, confirm in us the desire of our hearts to work and speak and think for you. May we use all our gifts in service to your children, in the spirit of Jesus. Amen.

OCTOBER 21, 1979

READ FROM YOUR BIBLE: PSALM 92:12-15.

The Lord Is My Rock

In 1933, Hitler came to power. To many Germans, he seemed to be a prophet. Others saw him as the door to destruction. Among those who opposed him from the beginning was a young minister who was teaching at the University of Berlin. This young man saw Hitler as one who was trying to make history without God. He went to England and served as pastor of two churches. In his sermons and conversation, he condemned the new government of his homeland because it had made Hitler its idol and god.

In 1935, he returned to Germany. There he began teaching in a training college for ministers. Because he called his pupils to return to the Bible and to oppose any

26

person or movement that tried to replace the living God, the college was closed in 1940 by the Gestapo.

When the second World War broke out, his friends tried to get him to leave Germany because he was opposed to serving in the army. For a short time, he came to the United States, but he soon returned to Germany since he felt he should be active in the struggle against Hitler. He became active in the political underground movement.

On April 5, 1943, he was arrested. In the years that followed, he was confined in several concentration camps. His courage, his unselfishness, and his goodness impressed not only other prisoners, but his guards as well. The guards became so attached to him that they smuggled out his writings and poems and apologized because they had to lock his cell.

His ministry was especially important to sick prisoners and those who were facing death sentences. He had an amazing ability to comfort those who were anxious or depressed. During the heavy air raids on Berlin, he was calm when other prisoners were beside themselves with fear.

On April 9, 1945, two years after he was imprisoned, and as the end of the war was near, he was shot on order of Himmler. He was a few months past his thirty-ninth birthday. The writings of this man—whose name was Dietrich Bonhoeffer—have inspired many Christians who have come to know them through books published after the war.

In the portion of the psalm we have heard today, the writer says that "the righteous will flourish like a palm tree." We usually think of flourishing as meaning that a person is rich in material things. But here the psalmist is thinking of flourishing as growth, not prosperity.

For the young German pastor, flourishing meant growth in faith and understanding of the love of God. In these, he found a happiness and peace that enabled him to withstand the fear and depression that afflicted so many who were in prison.

He also discovered that it was not enough to follow Christ by preaching and teaching. He was convinced that being a

Christian calls a person to action and self-sacrifice. He believed also that only those who gave up trying to prove that they were religious and who threw themselves upon the grace of God could be called Christians.

The psalm ends by saying that God is our rock. In a concentration camp or in any situation we face today, every one needs a rock. Life is filled with uncertainty. We never know what tomorrow will bring.

On the day before he was shot, Bonhoeffer conducted a worship service in prison. Many of those who attended were freed by the Allies soon afterward, and they spoke of the young pastor's calmness and sincerity. His last hours before he was taken away were spent in trying to comfort others. God was his rock.

Let us pray:

Jesus, Lord, we look to you to be our rock in every hour of need. We pray that we may be of one heart and mind, free from anger and pride. In your name. Amen.

OCTOBER 28, 1979

READ FROM YOUR BIBLE: I PETER 1:3-9.

Tested by Fire

Before the time of laws—and in some primitive countries today—the guilt or innocence of an individual suspected of a crime was tested through a process called the ordeal. It was based on a belief in magic, a belief that God would intervene in behalf of the innocent and would not allow a person who was not guilty to be harmed.

The ordeal was practiced in many forms. In the second century, the ordeal of bread and cheese was used. The person suspected of a crime was required to eat a sandwich made of communion bread and cheese. If the accused person were guilty, people thought God would send the angel Gabriel to stop his throat and he would not be able to swallow. Any person who could not eat the entire sandwich was judged to be guilty and punished according to his crime.

In the Middle Ages, ordeal by fire was used. A bonfire would be built and the accused person forced to walk through it, like the three godly men in the book of Daniel—Shadrach, Meshach, and Abednego (Daniel 3:12-30). If the person was not burned, he was believed to be innocent. If he were guilty, the fire itself would punish him. Another form of ordeal by fire required the accused person to carry a red hot iron for several steps.

Ordeal by water was also used. The people believed that water would reject a guilty person—in other words, the person would float—but that an innocent person would sink. The practice was to bind the person's hands to his feet and throw him into a pond or river. We may suspect that most persons sank and were therefore believed to be innocent—but because they were bound and could not swim, they drowned.

The ordeal existed in Europe until the thirteenth century, when it was condemned by the church. Gradually, the idea of law courts grew. Witnesses gave testimony under oath, and a sworn jury became the judge of facts.

The ordeal must have been a fearful instrument, and many innocent people were punished by this primitive system. Humanity made a great leap forward when the rule of law emerged.

In our scripture reading for today, Peter warned the followers of Christ that they would have to suffer many trials. Their faith, like gold, would be tested by fire.

In fact, many early Christians were tested by fire as were the apostles. They were crucified, thrown to wild beasts, burned, and buried alive. To be a Christian in the Roman empire during the first three hundred years after the death and resurrection of Christ required that a person be ready to die in faithfulness. People believed that any person who

29

died in defense of the Christian faith would go immediately to heaven.

Peter tells Christians in the letter we have read today that they have been "born anew to a living hope through the resurrection of Jesus Christ from the dead." If they are faithful, they will receive "an inheritance which is imperishable, undefiled, and unfading." The outcome of this faith is the salvation of one's soul.

In the church today, we know very little persecution. In most communities, a Christian is the thing to be. Even so, we may find that our commitment to Christ is weak and our faith ineffective. We may be timid and embarrassed and fail to make a faithful witness to Christ.

When we see a lack of vitality in our faith and think of the Christians who so freely gave their lives through the ordeal of fire, we should be ashamed. Peter has told us in his letter of the stakes. We must listen attentively to his words to the first generation of Christians and follow their example. He wrote: "Without seeing him you love him; though you do not now see him you believe in him and rejoice with unutterable and exalted joy. As the outcome of your faith you obtain the salvation of your souls."

Let us pray:

Almighty God, who sees that we have no power in ourselves, aid us in making a true and faithful witness in the world. May we be inspired by those early martyrs who were tested in fire, to the end that we shall win the crown of life, through your son. Amen.

All Things United in God

Following the beginning of the Protestant Reformation, which got under way in the 1500s, some Christians felt the reforms of the church had not gone far enough. These people were called Puritans, and some of them came to America and set up the Massachusetts Bay Colony. Other people felt that even the Puritans had not gone far enough. They wanted to get back to the simplicity of the early church.

One of these reformers was George Fox. In about 1647, Fox began preaching that true disciples of Christ were those whose lives were wholly changed through the power of the Holy Spirit. For the Christian, this inward Spirit was a source of strength and guidance in practical affairs. The people who gathered around Fox and followed his teachings were called the Society of Friends, or, as most people know them, Quakers.

The Quaker movement grew rapidly and soon spread to America. In the year 1656, two women who were Quakers landed in Boston. They were charged with holding dangerous opinions and put in jail. Their books were burned, and they were shipped away to the West Indies. Only two days after they sailed, eight more Quakers arrived from England. They too were put in jail, and they were sent back to London three months later.

Other Quakers continued to come to the American colonies. They were often whipped, put in jail, and banished. Between 1659 and 1661, four Quakers were hanged.

In England also, Quakers were persecuted. More than fourteen thousand were fined and put in prison, and three hundred sixty-nine died in English jails. But by the end of the century, persecution had ended. Quakers became a

31

respected religious group and were active in missionary work.

What was truly remarkable about these early Quakers was their unity of Spirit. Though they were few in number, they made an impact on the communities where they lived because they were so sincere in their faith. They were among the first people to call for equal rights for women, education for Indians, reform of prisons, better treatment for the insane, and the abolition of slavery. Although they were mistreated for their views, they stood firmly united in Christ.

In the passage we have heard today from the first chapter of Ephesians, Paul speaks of the spiritual blessing we have in Christ. According to the will of God, we are redeemed by grace through the forgiveness of our sins. It is in Christ that the unity of things in heaven and on earth are found.

All Christians, such as the Quakers who were so persecuted for their faith, receive the spiritual blessings promised by God. He enriches our lives in many ways through spiritual gifts. As we seek a personal relationship with God through Jesus Christ, we are filled with his presence and power. It is through this personal relationship that the Quakers and others who have been persecuted find the will to live by the inward light and presence of the spirit of Christ. It is this personal relationship that gave them their sense of unity with Christ and with one another.

In the broken world in which we live today, we seek some experience that will bring harmony and unity to our lives. According to the teaching of the New Testament, it is the spirit of God that unites us. To receive this spirit does not require anything of us except humility and an open heart. The presence of the Spirit in the lives of men and women is a part of God's eternal purpose.

Our response to this gift should be "praise of his glorious grace which he freely bestowed on us." By this grace, we shall also experience the unity of God in which all things come together.

32

Let us pray:

Blessed Lord, as the days of life hasten on, inspire us with love and zeal. Especially do we pray for that unity of spirit that binds us to you and to one another. For the sake of Christ. Amen.

NOVEMBER 11, 1979
READ FROM YOUR BIBLE: EPHESIANS 3:7-13.

The Least of All the Saints

In Arlington National Cemetery, across the Potomac River from Washington, D. C., is a spot visited each year by thousands of Americans. It was established in 1921, and it is known as the Tomb of the Unknown Soldier.

In that year, Congress passed a resolution to bring home from France the body of one of the nearly two thousand soldiers killed in the first World War and never identified. The process for selecting the unknown soldier was detailed. The United States had four cemeteries in France where unknown soldiers were buried. One casket was brought from each of these cemeteries to a central place near the French battlefields. The caskets were placed in one room, all shipping records were destroyed, and the caskets rearranged several times by different groups of soldiers so that no one knew from which cemetery any of the caskets had come.

On October 24, 1921, an American sergeant was sent into the room to choose which of the unknowns would be brought back to the United States. He walked around the caskets three times, then placed a rose on the coffin he selected.

The body of that soldier was returned to the United States aboard a navy ship. After it docked in Washington, the casket was taken to the Capitol where it lay in state for two days. Thousands of Americans walked past it in honor of all those who had died in the war.

On November 11, 1921, Armistice Day, three years after the war had ended, the unknown soldier was buried in a tomb as President Warren G. Harding and thousands watched. The president conferred on this unknown soldier the Medal of Honor in behalf of a grateful nation.

On Memorial Day in 1958, as President Eisenhower watched, two other unknowns, representing those who died in the second World War and the Korean War, were buried in the tomb.

Of these persons whose bodies now symbolize our honored dead from all wars, probably not one of them would have thought of himself as a hero. Like millions of others, each of these unknowns was only doing his duty. Modestly, he probably thought of himself as the apostle Paul thought of himself, as "the very least of all the saints." The millions who have seen the tomb since 1921, however, highly regard the three who are buried there as symbols of the brave men and women who have fought the good fight for freedom.

In the passage from Ephesians we have heard today, Paul, who was a real martyr and hero, calls himself "the very least of all the saints." He did not see himself as a great missionary, for he gave all the honor to Christ. He saw Christ as the fulfillment of God's eternal purpose. Through God's wisdom, "the unsearchable riches of Christ" had been given. Paul humbly rejoiced at the grace of God in his life, even though he was in prison in Rome.

If so great a Christian as Paul was humble, how much more should we show humility. Humility is mentioned often in the New Testament. Jesus himself is the prime example. At no time in his ministry, even during the ordeal of his trial and crucifixion, did he lose his sense of humility. We find no trace of pride or arrogance in his life or teaching.

Humility is the key to peace and harmony in the Christian community. Pride and arrogance show a lack of concern for others, a feeling that one is better or more deserving than one's brothers and sisters in faith.

Prestige and power are major issues in human society, for in our institutions they are related to authority. In the Christian fellowship, all authority belongs to God.

As we work toward maturity in our Christian experience, we look to the example of Christ and Paul. We should see ourselves in humility as "the very least of all the saints."

Let us pray:

Dear Master, forgive us for those thoughts of pride and arrogance that sometimes creep into our minds. May we look to Calvary to see the image of your humility and may we model our lives after Christ. In your spirit we pray. Amen.

NOVEMBER 18, 1979
READ FROM YOUR BIBLE: EPHESIANS 5:15-20.

Look at How You Walk

In the spring of 1978, several hundred American Indians set out from California to walk to Washington, D. C. In July, they arrived. They called their pilgrimage "the longest walk."

It began in Sacramento, California, on February 11 with several hundred marchers. For several months, the group moved slowly eastward. Along the way, some Indians dropped out, but others joined. By July, as the group neared Washington, a caravan of cars, vans, and pickup trucks from many states joined with the one thousand marchers.

On "the longest walk," the Indians slept in schools, churches, gyms, and fairgrounds. One sixteen-year-old boy who walked the entire distance said he had worn out five or six pairs of shoes.

Why would a group walk so far? They were trying to get public attention focused on the problems faced by American Indians in this country.

The Indians claim that they have been treated unfairly. Their treaties have been broken time after time, and their lands and resources have been taken from them. Many times Congress has changed Indian treaties at will because Indians have had no power to resist.

At the time the Indians made their march, bills were before Congress that would have repealed all existing Indian treaties; closed all Indian hospitals, schools, and housing projects; done away with Indian fishing and hunting rights; abolished the Bureau of Indian Affairs; and ended the special relationship Indians have had with the United States government.

So the Indians came to Washington. Hundreds of them camped in state parks in nearby Maryland, while Indian leaders lived in a sacred compound near the Lincoln Memorial. There the perpetual fire burned, and religious ceremonies were carried out. The walk had been peaceful, but Congress and the American people knew they were serious.

Paul tells the Ephesians that they must look carefully at how they walk. They must be watchful, cautious, wise. The Apostle tells them to look carefully. They should make the most of their time. Even though the days are evil and moral standards are low, they should not be foolish. They should seek out the will of God. They should not get drunk, for drunkenness suggests a life that is already far gone in its way toward ruin.

Paul urges the Ephesians to be filled with the spirit, and he suggests some of the ways in which spiritual life may grow and be enriched. Spiritual depth will be increased as Christians join in fellowship, in "singing and making melody to the Lord with all your heart" (Ephesians 5:19).

Above all, they should "for everything" give "thanks in the name of our Lord Jesus Christ to God the Father" (Ephesians 5:20).

Paul's summary of the Christian life as he gives it to us here may be stated simply.
• Be careful about the way you walk or live.
• Make the most of your time.
• Understand the will of God.
• Be filled with the Spirit.
• Make melody to the Lord with all your heart.
• Give thanks to God for everything.

American Indians in the summer of 1978 called attention to their concerns through what they called "the longest walk," from California to the nation's capital. We may call attention to our commitment to be Christian witnesses by the way we walk. How are you walking as a follower of Christ?

Let us pray:

O Son of God, help us to be aware of our walk before the world. Forgive us when we bring dishonor to you and to fellow Christians by the way we walk. Amen.

NOVEMBER 25, 1979
READ FROM YOUR BIBLE: EPHESIANS 2:1-10.

Made Alive in Christ

On the night of August 15, 1978, there was an air of tenseness in Memphis, Tennessee. The city had been left with reduced police and fire protection for a week because of a strike of policemen and firemen. In addition, thousands of Elvis Presley fans had gathered in Memphis on the first anniversary of the singer's death.

Just after midnight, the entire city was plunged into darkness. Almost immediately, looting began in various parts of the city. Shelves in many stores were cleaned out while Memphis was without light.

The next day, the story of what had happened came out. A security guard at a power substation had been drinking before he came on duty. He was not supposed to go inside the fence, but someone had left the gate to the substation unlocked, and the security guard went inside. For reasons he could not later explain, he began throwing switches. In all, he pulled seven switches. When power went out in the area near the substation, the demand for power was increased at a nearby steam plant. The overload was so great that power went out over the entire city.

In Memphis on that August night, nearly seven hundred thousand people were thrown into darkness. Since the police were on strike, people were afraid. They had no idea what might happen next.

In the hours that followed the total blackout of the city, the supervisor of the security guards arrived at the substation where the switches had been pulled. The guard on duty seemed intoxicated. The supervisor began questioning him and the man confessed that he had pulled down seven switches.

Power officials soon arrived and turned the switches back to their "on" position. Once again, Memphis was a lighted city.

The scripture passage we have heard today is part of the section in which Paul prays for the enlightenment of his readers. The word "enlightenment" suggests the bringing of light, and Paul here talks about God giving light to humanity through Christ.

Even more important, Paul speaks of death and life. Here death means following Satan in a life of sin. The power of evil pushes in on every aspect of human life. The temptation to put oneself first and overlook obedience to God and the needs of others is ever present. The "sons of disobedience" mentioned here refers to all unbelief. The desires of the flesh are not gross physical sins so much as conduct that grows out of a lack of principle. This life that is under the sway of the power of evil is the same as death, for it has no future.

BUT . . . "God, who is rich in mercy, out of the great love with which he loved us, even when we were dead through our trespasses, made us alive together with Christ" (2:4-5). God brought us from darkness to light, from death to life. Those who have faith in Christ are raised from the state of death caused by sin to heavenly places, and this experience of being raised is shared by both Christ and all other Christians.

Another idea Paul presents here under inspiration of the Holy Spirit is that of eternity. Eternity is understood as meaning in the coming ages. In that unending future, God will continue to "show the immeasurable riches of his grace in kindness toward us in Christ Jesus."

How are we made alive in Christ? By faith. Paul tells us that we are saved from death—from Satan who plunges us into a life of darkness like the security guard plunged the city of Memphis into darkness. God through Christ has brought us into the light, rescued us from our sins and death, and raised us to sit with him in heavenly places.

Let us pray:

God of the ages, strengthen us in our fight against the power of evil in the world today. Keep us watchful, keep us strong through the full depth of your mercy. In the spirit of our Savior. Amen.

––––––––––––

DECEMBER 2, 1979
READ FROM YOUR BIBLE: ISAIAH 40:21-26.

To Whom Will We Compare God?

When we look at the sky on a clear, dark night, we see thousands of twinkling lights in the sky. Until a few centuries ago, the stars and planets were thought to be distant lights scattered over a dome called "the heavens." The earth was thought to be the center of the whole universe. The sun, moon, and stars seemed to be revolving about our planet.

As far back as four centuries before the time of Christ, some Greeks thought that the earth revolved around the sun, but few people accepted the idea. After all, a person couldn't feel the earth revolving—common sense indicated that the earth was still—so the other objects in the heavens, including the sun, must be moving around the earth.

More than five hundred years ago, Copernicus, an astronomer in Poland, published a book in which he said that the earth moved around the sun. His work was carried on by a brilliant German mathematician by the name of Kepler. His theories paved the way for our modern understanding of the universe.

John (his German name was Johannes) Kepler was born in the year 1571. His interest in studying the universe was aroused when he was in college. He was a brilliant young man, and his teachers thought at the time that he had such a magnificent mind that something special could be expected from him. Although he was a young scientist of unusual mental gifts, his real interest lay in religion. He intended to become a minister. In 1594, when the teacher of math at a church school died, Kepler was asked to become his replacement.

Only a year later, when he was twenty-four years old, he hit upon what he believed to be the key to the secret of the universe. In the summer of 1595, twenty-five years before the Pilgrims landed at Plymouth, Kepler studied the problem with the whole energy of his mind. He spent hours and hours trying to understand the relationship of the planets in terms of their number, size, and orbits. One day in July, as he was teaching his class, an idea suddenly struck him of how he might prove by mathematics that Copernicus was right. For several days and nights, he carried on his calculations. Within a few days, he had worked out the formulas showing how our solar system fits together.

The next year Kepler published a book on his findings. In it he said that at the beginning of his work he had prayed that God would help him discover whether Copernicus was right. Although he had wanted to be a theologian, he had found a way to celebrate God's creation through studying the stars. He wrote that Providence had helped him, for he would never have found the solution to the puzzle of the solar system by his own efforts. Behind man's theories of creation lay the God who had made the universe.

The scripture reading we have heard today helps us compare the greatness and majesty of God with the smallness of humans on the planet earth. God is the Lord of nature.

> It is he who sits above the circle of the earth,
>   and its inhabitants are like grasshoppers;
> who stretches out the heavens like a curtain,
>   and spreads them like a tent to dwell in;
> who brings princes to nought,
>   and makes the rulers of the earth as nothing.
>   (Isaiah 40:22-23)

From where God sits, we are like grasshoppers. Let's think of that a moment. If you are walking in your yard or garden or field on a summer day, you may notice a grasshopper jumping near you in the grass. But when you are gone away from that spot, do you think again of the grasshopper? Probably not. Do you think about whether that grasshopper will live or perish? Probably not. Will you wonder if that grasshopper has any hope for a better day tomorrow? Probably not.

When we think of how great God is and how small we are, we may begin to feel the wonder John Kepler felt when he discovered how the planets, including the earth, relate to the sun. The solar system and the universe are awesome in their size. The laws by which the universe operates are complex. Some stars are so far away that it takes billions of years for their light to get to the earth. Do we not feel a sense of awe when we compare our smallness to the size of God's creation?

41

Yet this wondrous Creator made us and loves us. Unlike our attitude toward the grasshopper or cricket, he is concerned about us. He wants our lives to be filled with meaning. Most of all, he wants us to come to him through his son, Jesus Christ.

To whom can we compare God? To no one. His majesty we cannot grasp. But we are grateful that he has drawn near us through Christ and that he is near us today.

Let us pray:

Father, in whom we live, in whom we are and move, let us render thanks to you for the world you have given us for a home. But most of all, we give you thanks for your redeeming grace and renewing power. In Christ's name. Amen.

DECEMBER 9, 1979

READ FROM YOUR BIBLE: ROMANS 5:1-11.

The Promise of Salvation

On a Monday night in May of last year, a large airliner was preparing to land at Pensacola, Florida, in a dense fog. Passengers expected to see the plane touch down at any moment.

The plane touched down, but the people on board discovered to their horror that they were not on the runway, but in the water of the bay next to the airport. One person later told reporters that he thought the plane was on land until he felt the water pouring in around his feet.

In the first moments, the passengers were almost too shocked to react. Then cries of "Help me! Save me!" began to be heard. The exits were opened, and some people were able to climb to the top of the airplane. Because the fog was so thick, they had no idea how far they were from land. Most of them probably thought that death was only minutes away.

What happened next seemed like a miracle. As they peered out into the darkness, passengers saw a tugboat only a few hundred feet away. The tugboat captain turned his craft toward the airplane, and in a few minutes he was pulling people out of the choppy water. They first lifted out those who had not had time to put on their life jackets. Then they moved nearer the airplane and laid a plank from the plane to the boat for other passengers to cross. Only three passengers drowned; fifty-five were saved.

What seemed most remarkable was the fact that the tugboat captain said he was lost himself when he saw the plane in the water. An officer of the marine patrol said that many more lives would have been lost if the tugboat had not been nearby when the plane hit the water three miles from the airport. The passengers on the plane must have felt doomed to death until the boat appeared to save them.

The scripture reading we have heard today is the beginning of a section in the book of Romans on the new life in Christ. Some Christians would say that chapters five through eight of Romans are the most important of all the writings of Paul. In earlier chapters of this book, the great apostle has been writing about justification by faith. The writer tells us that justification is the door to salvation. It leads to a new life as the believer comes to accept God's promises of forgiveness and renewed fellowship with him.

Paul goes on to describe the features of this new life. In the first place, we have peace with God through Jesus Christ. It is through Christ that we have access to grace and the hope of sharing the glory of God. The love of God has been poured into our hearts through the Holy Spirit.

Paul continues his explanation of the act of Christ. We were helpless because we could not atone for our own sin. Then Christ died for us. Although someone might die for a good person, one would scarcely expect that degree of sacrifice. When Christ died for us, God showed his love for us while we were yet sinners. Though we may have been enemies of God before, through the death of his son we are now reconciled to him, and it is through Christ that we have received this reconciliation.

This scripture reading tells us that it is through Christ that we too are reunited with God. This act of reunion is all God's work. He begins it, and he carries it out. According to Paul, we cannot help ourselves. Only God can help with a problem so deep. We had become separated from God through our sin. Our relationship with our heavenly Father was shattered. We were hostile toward God, but he took the step to bring us back to himself through his son.

The rich life of fellowship with God is now open to us. He has fulfilled his promise of salvation. When we think on it, the reality of this promise seems a miracle to us. At the right time, when the big airliner fell into Pensacola Bay, the tugboat was nearby. People who thought they would soon be lost were saved.

In a similar way, when all humanity seemed lost, God sent his son at the right time. Though we are ungodly, Christ died for us. Today he holds out to us the promise of a new life in Jesus Christ.

Let us pray:

Eternal God and sovereign Lord, we pause at this moment to become aware again of the promise of your salvation. It is too lofty for us to understand. Accept our thanks, we pray, in the name of Jesus Christ. Amen.

DECEMBER 16, 1979
READ FROM YOUR BIBLE: COLOSSIANS 3:12-17.

The Peace of Christ

One of the saddest events in the Old Testament is the tragedy of King David and his son Absalom. Absalom was

44

one of his father's favorites, but he plotted for the king's power. At the town of Hebron, not far from Jerusalem where King David lived, Absalom had himself declared king. When this news came to David, his servants told him he should leave Jerusalem immediately, for Absalom might try to kill him.

David and his loyal followers left Jerusalem. Going out past the Mount of Olives—where Jesus was to suffer in the hours before his trial and crucifixion nearly a thousand years later—David wept as he walked along, barefoot and with his head covered in mourning. How sad he must have been over the fact that his beloved son was driving him off the throne and out of the city.

Soon after David left, Absalom and his followers came to Jerusalem and Absalom moved into the king's house. One of Absalom's officials urged him to send an army after his father. He said David would be weary and discouraged and could easily be killed. Another official urged Absalom to wait until the people were solidly behind him. Meanwhile, David and his followers fled east across the Jordan River.

Later, Absalom gathered an army and went in pursuit of his father. David also sent his army to meet his son's, but he told the three commanders: " 'Deal gently for my sake with the young man Absalom' " (2 Samuel 18:5). Soon the armies met in a forest. Absalom was riding through the woods on a mule, and his head caught on the branches of an oak tree. The mule went on, leaving Absalom hanging in midair.

One of David's commanders heard of this and went to the place where Absalom was caught in the tree. He struck Absalom, and other soldiers joined in to kill Absalom. The news was taken to David, who was sitting at the city gate, waiting to hear the outcome of the battle. When the messenger arrived, David asked, " 'Is it well with the young man Absalom?' " (2 Samuel 18:32). The messenger had to tell him that his son was dead. The old king went to a room over the gate and wept, saying, " 'O my son Absalom, my son, my son Absalom! Would I had died instead of you, O Absalom, my son, my son.' "

When parent and child become enemies, tragedy is the

result. How many parents have suffered because of some action of their child. And how many children have been abused and mistreated by their parents. Love and respect should be the marks of the relationship between parent and child.

In the scripture lesson we have read today, we are told that the peace of Christ should rule in our hearts. The church has been called "the family of God." The church is made up of our brothers and sisters in Christ. These brothers and sisters in God's family are called "God's chosen ones" (Colossians 3:12).

What are the characteristics of God's chosen ones? The apostle Paul tells us here that we are to put on "compassion, kindness, lowliness, meekness, and patience, forbearing one another and, if one has a complaint against another, forgiving each other" (Colossians 3:12-13).

Sometimes strife may occur in the church, the family of God. As in the household of David, one person may want the place held by another. Unless the peace of Christ is brought into such a situation, a tragedy may occur, just as in the case of David and Absalom. In the case of this father and son, it is ironic that the name Absalom means "father of peace." In this case, the child was the father of strife, not peace.

Paul calls us to remember that we are one body. As in a human body, one member cannot war against another, but all parts of the body must work together in harmony.

As brothers and sisters in Christ, we are called to walk in a transformed life. The bitterness of competition must be laid aside and replaced by humility and a desire to serve. We are to teach and admonish each other with thankfulness in our hearts. "And whatever you do, in word or deed, do everything in the name of the Lord Jesus, giving thanks to God the Father through him" (Colossians 3:17).

Let us pray:

Wondrous Lord, help us as we try to make our group a part of your family. Fill our lives with a sense of your divine presence until your will becomes our will. Through Jesus Christ our Lord. Amen.

READ FROM YOUR BIBLE: LUKE 1:26-35.

God's Promises Never Fail

As we come near the celebration of Christmas, we are drawn again to the story of the birth of Jesus. Our scripture lesson tells of God's promise to Mary that she should bear a son. In her surprise, Mary could not believe this word of revelation and promise that she received from the angel Gabriel.

In the Old Testament, we find another account of the promise of a son and the disbelief that followed. The book of Genesis tells the story of Abraham and Sarah, his wife. Abraham and his family had settled in the land of Canaan after God had promised to give him that land and descendants as numerous as grains of sand and stars in the sky. But Abraham and Sarah had no children, and they were already old people.

One day as Abraham and Sarah were sitting in the opening of their tent, three men approached. Abraham offered them food. Before they left, one of the strangers said that Abraham and Sarah would have a son. When Sarah laughed, because she was past the age of bearing children, and Abraham was almost a hundred years old, the visitor replied, "Is anything too hard for the Lord?" (Genesis 18:14).

About a year later, Abraham and Sarah became parents, and they named their son Isaac.

After some time God tested Abraham. He told him to take Isaac, the son of his old age, to the land of Moriah, which is believed to be the name of the hill where the temple would later stand in Jerusalem. God told Abraham that he was to kill Isaac and offer him as a sacrifice.

Because Abraham trusted God and was obedient, he took his son as God directed. When they got to the place,

47

Abraham built an altar of sacrifice, arranged wood on it, bound his son, and laid him on the altar. As he raised his knife and prepared to kill his son, he heard a voice that commanded him to stop. He had proved that he was a God-fearing man, ready to offer his son if God required it.

Almost two thousand years later, a holy child was promised to Mary. He was to be called Jesus, and he would be the Son of God. "How can this be?" asked Mary, for she had no husband. The angel answered just as the stranger had responded to Sarah. "With God nothing will be impossible" (Luke 1:37).

Two women—Sarah and Mary—were promised a son under unusual circumstances. The promises were fulfilled. God spared the son of Sarah, but his own son gave his life upon the cross.

As we near the day in the year when we celebrate the birth of Jesus, we remember that this child born in a manger in Bethlehem would someday be crucified in Jerusalem, only five miles from his birthplace and near the place where Isaac was offered by his father, Abraham. In all the pleasure and excitement of Christmas, we may easily forget the destiny of the baby who was promised to Mary.

When we remember that the baby in Bethlehem would someday be the victim of the cross, we may develop a better perspective on the meaning of Christmas. Although God wants his people to be joyful, we are reminded that life brings to us many different experiences. Along with joy, we also have somber moments. The true meaning of Christmas is lost if we fail to see during these days the whole life of Jesus. From the Christian viewpoint, we celebrate his birth in part because of the meaning of his life and death. The baby born at Bethlehem was different from every other baby in the destiny that he had to fulfill.

During this holiday, let us take a few moments from time to time to remember the true meaning of this day. While we celebrate the babe of Bethlehem, let's remember also the Savior who died and rose again.

48

Let us pray:

O Lord, our Lord, how excellent is your name. As the day of celebration grows near, may we be reminded that your promises never fail. We join the heavenly hosts today to magnify your name. Amen.

DECEMBER 30, 1979

READ FROM YOUR BİBLE: ISAIAH 40:3-8.

Preparing the Way

On September 21, 1791, Michael Faraday was born into the family of a poor English blacksmith. His father, James Faraday, was in such poor health that he was often unable to work. Once young Michael was given a loaf of bread and told that was all the food he would have for a week.

Michael had little opportunity for an education, but he became one of the most famous men of his time. He was the man who discovered how to make an electric motor. The motors that drive machines in our industries and in our homes today are a part of the contribution of Michael Faraday.

By the time he was thirteen years old, he had barely learned to read, write, and do simple arithmetic. But at that age, he began work by delivering newspapers. A year later he started learning the trade of bookbinding. While he was binding books, he would often read parts of them. He happened to read a book by Isaac Watts, who preached and wrote hymns, such as, "O God Our Help in Ages Past."

The book by Watts was on self-improvement. Young Michael began to follow the advice of the author by keeping a notebook in which he wrote his ideas. He helped a discussion group get started that was devoted to the exchange of ideas. He also began attending lectures of all kinds, and he wrote many facts and observations made by these speakers in his notebook. In this way, he began to develop a questioning mind that would later serve him well.

The other important aspect of his early life was his religious faith. The church he attended with his parents stressed reading the Bible and the love and sense of community of the early church. These features were a part of his daily life. A friend and associate later said that he believed Faraday's scientific strength and energy arose out of his regular church attendance.

One day when Faraday was rebinding a volume of the *Encyclopedia Brittanica,* he happened to read an article on electricity. He began to try some experiments of his own, and, from that time onward, his chief ambition was to become a scientist. Working all day binding books, he had little opportunity to learn because there were no night schools, public libraries, or correspondence courses.

A turning point in his life came when he joined a discussion group devoted to science. The group met each week, and Faraday listened with attention and made careful notes. But there seemed to be little likelihood that he would ever become more than a bookbinder with an interest in science.

Through a chance misfortune, his life was changed. One of the most important scientists of the day was blinded temporarily by an accident. Michael Faraday was recommended to help the scientist while his eyes healed. When he regained his sight, he hired the young Faraday to stay on as his assistant.

The remainder of his life story is now part of the history of modern science. He discovered benzene in 1825 and in 1831 he discovered the principle that made possible the building of an electric motor. Not only was he famous as a discoverer; he was also known as a brilliant speaker on science. He even gave lectures to children to increase their interest in science.

Faraday's early life prepared the way for him to become a famous scientist. His religious faith provided an inner strength. Though his family was poor, they believed in love and community. Though he had very little formal schooling, he took advantage of every opportunity to learn on his own.

The scripture reading we have heard today is also about preparation or preparing the way. In ancient times, a new road would sometimes be prepared for a king. The prophet Isaiah uses this image and cries, "Prepare the way of the Lord as if preparing the way for the coming of a king." A new kingdom was to begin. God would reveal himself as his purposes were fulfilled. Though grass will wither and flowers will fade, "the word of our God will stand forever" (Isaiah 40:8).

As we come to the end of one year and the beginning of a new one, we listen eagerly to God's promise. Not only will his word stand forever, but also his son, whose birth we celebrated a few days ago, is our savior forever. Let us give thanks for his gift.

May we also at the beginning of this new year prepare the way in our hearts for a new revelation of the power of God.

Let us pray:

Our gracious Master and our God, as we pass to a new year from an old one, we beg for your presence in the year that lies ahead. We pray for life and health and peace. Through Jesus Christ our Lord. Amen.

JANUARY 6, 1980

READ FROM YOUR BIBLE: MARK 2:18-22.

No Time for Mourning

In 1973, a musical event of great importance took place—a professional pianist who had disappeared from view in the 1920's was rediscovered. Now an old man who had not owned a piano or practiced in over forty years, he sat down at a concert piano in a Presbyterian church in San Francisco and, without even looking at the music, played in a way that amazed those who came to hear him.

He was born in Hungary and gave his first public concert when he was six years old. When he was only seventeen, he came to America and played at Carnegie Hall. He liked this country so much that he decided to stay here.

Soon, however, he vanished from public view. He went to California and played musical scores for United Artists, a difficult task that sometimes required reading fifteen lines of music at a glance. He was married and divorced several times, but he never played the piano publicly unless he needed money. In 1973, he was rediscovered.

In recent years, he had not practiced at all. He said that after he had played a piece two or three times, he would have it memorized. Today he can still play from memory more than a thousand piano works, many of them extremely difficult and several pages in length.

He was a "wonderchild." When he was only eight years old, he read all of Shakespeare's works in German. By the time he was twelve, he was playing piano with the Berlin Philharmonic.

In spite of his rediscovery, he still lives in a poor district of San Francisco. He has written more than seven hundred piano compositions of his own, but he never plays them in public. He spends his days reading books on philosophy and drama.

When asked how he felt about those years when he was lost from public view and his name forgotten by those who heard him in the 1920's, he said he did not dwell on "what might have been." Even if he could live his life over, he said he would probably make the same mistakes. Then he smiled and said, "But there have been great moments too." In other words, there is no time for mourning.

The passage from the Gospel of Mark that we have read today comes from Jesus' early ministry in Galilee. His healing ministry had already begun and was attracting attention. The scribes and Pharisees were angry because he claimed to forgive sins. They believed that not even the messiah could forgive sins; only God could do that. They were watching Jesus to see what else he might do so they could bring a charge of blasphemy against him. Blasphemy was the charge for any act that seemed irreverent toward God.

In the Bible, fasting and abstaining from food or drink was practiced on many occasions. On the Day of Atonement, for instance, Jews were not to eat or drink from morning until evening. The other occasions when Jews fasted were times of distress such as war, sickness, mourning, penitence, impending danger, or drought.

In the passage we have heard, we learn that John the Baptist had taught his disciples to fast, probably as a sign of penitence for their sins. The Pharisees also fasted, following the customs of the Old Testament.

The people came to Jesus to ask why his disciples did not fast. His response was that since the kingdom of God was at hand it was no time for mourning. It was rather a time for celebration, like a wedding feast. At a time of joy, no one wants to fast.

This note of joy plays a central part in the teaching of Jesus. The word "joy" appears in the New Testament more than fifty times.

What is the place of joy in the Christian life today? For E. Stanley Jones, the great missionary to India in this century, joy was an essential part of the Christian life.

We ask ourselves, therefore, about our sense of joy in the Christian life and fellowship. For some Christians, there seems to be little joy. Their faith seems to call forth mourning and sadness. Such followers of Christ may not be effective in drawing others into the Christian faith. Today our world is desperate for joy. Let us be joyful disciples in order that others may be drawn into our fellowship with Christ.

Let us pray:

Hear, O Lord, our pleas as we touch and handle things unseen. Let us grasp with a firmer hand the grace you have offered us, and may we experience true joy. Through Jesus Christ our Lord. Amen.

READ FROM YOUR BIBLE: ROMANS 6:1-11.

United in Christ

Wednesday, February 7, 1894, was an unusual holiday in the southern Mississippi town of Columbia. Early in the morning, families began to gather on the courthouse lawn with picnic lunches. The occasion for the holiday was the hanging of Will Purvis.

In June of the previous year, Will Buckley, a prominent farmer in Columbia, had talked to a grand jury about the activities of "The White Caps," a secret group like the Ku Klux Klan. Nearly everybody knew that Buckley's life had been threatened if he talked to the grand jury. On his way home that day, he was ambushed and killed.

The man who was finally charged with the murder was Will Purvis. He was a hardworking young man, twenty years old, who helped his father on their one hundred twenty acre farm. Although witnesses said they saw him working on the farm at the time of the murder, he was convicted and sentenced to be hanged. After the judge sentenced him, Purvis looked at the members of the jury and quietly said, "I'll outlive every one of you."

After repeated appeals had been lost, the time came for the sheriff to prepare the gallows. On the night before the hanging was to take place, heavy weights were suspended from the rope to be sure that it would not break. On the morning of the execution, five thousand people gathered on the lawn of the courthouse.

At the appointed hour, Purvis was taken from the jail and led up the steps to the gallows. A minister read a passage of scripture as the noose was placed around the neck of the convicted man. The sheriff then asked the prisoner if he had any last words. Purvis looked over the crowd and shouted, "I didn't do it." The sheriff sprang the trapdoor. Five thousand people sighed and groaned at what they saw.

Instead of hanging at the end of the rope, Will Purvis was lying on the ground under the gallows. The knot around his neck had completely unraveled!

The governor commuted his sentence to life imprisonment, and he was pardoned after he had served about five years in prison. He still insisted that he was innocent. Twenty-three years after that February day when they tried to hang Will Purvis, another man confessed to the district attorney that he had committed the crime with which Purvis had been charged. Before a grand jury could hear the man's confession, he died of pneumonia.

Will Purvis lived on to marry, become the father of eleven children, and own his own farm. After the confession of the real murderer, Purvis went to New York to appear on the radio. Hollywood made an offer to film a movie of his life, but he wasn't interested. On October 13, 1938, he died. No one told him, but perhaps he knew, that five days earlier the last of the jurors who had sentenced him to hang had died. He had made good his courtroom vow forty-five years before, that he would outlive every man on the jury that had convicted him.

In the lesson we have heard today from the sixth chapter of Romans, Paul was writing about our union with Christ. If we have died with him, "we shall certainly be united with him in a resurrection like his" (Romans 6:5). The certainty of resurrection is based in our confidence that Christ is our hope. The union we have with Christ makes us part of his risen life. We are no longer subject to the power of sin, because our old self was crucified with him. Slavery to sin has been overcome through his death. We are dead to sin and alive to God.

Will Purvis escaped from death when the noose unraveled on that February day in 1894, but in October of 1938 he faced death again. He was not afraid for, on the last day of his life, he said that he was ready to die. The Christian who is united with Christ through faith has no fear. United with Christ in death, we shall be united with him in resurrection.

55

Let us pray:

God, all merciful, we thank you for the promise that if we have died with Christ we shall be united in a resurrection like his. May we sense the victory we have over the power of sin, through Jesus Christ our Lord. Amen.

JANUARY 20, 1980

READ FROM YOUR BIBLE: PHILIPPIANS 2:3-11.

Christ Our Model

On a July day in 1969, a fourteen-year-old boy was frolicking in the ocean at a beach on the Oregon coast. The breakers were high, but, since he was having a good time, he didn't notice. Suddenly a big wave fell on him full force, and he was quickly carried by the current out into deep water.

Nearby, two young men, one a carpenter and the other an office clerk, had seen the boy playing in the water. Moments later, they saw him swept out to sea by the undertow. Almost instantly, both young men ran toward the water, taking off their shirts as they ran. Jumping into the ocean, they began to swim toward the boy, who by this time had been swept out more than three hundred feet from shore, where the water was twenty feet deep.

By the time they got to the boy, both young men were tired because of swimming through the breakers. Having come that far, however, they were determined to save him even at great danger to themselves. They each took one of the boy's arms and began swimming toward the shore.

Farther out to sea, two men in a motorboat had seen the rescue effort. They turned their boat toward the shore to help. Just as they got alongside the men and the boy, a huge wave crashed down on the three persons in the water. The boy came back up to the surface, but the two young men who had rescued him were never seen again. The men in the motorboat rushed the boy to the ambulance waiting on the beach. At the hospital, he was revived and he soon fully recovered.

What of the two young men, the carpenter and the clerk? Because of their rescue efforts, they were so tired that they had been swept out to sea by strong currents. Both young men drowned. Although they were both excellent swimmers, in their determination to save the boy they lost their own lives.

In our passage for today, Paul in writing to the Philippian church urges his readers to be "in full accord and of one mind"; they are to take on the mind of Christ.

To be of one mind does not mean everyone has to think exactly like everyone else; rather, it means having one goal or standard. For Christians it involves taking Christ's humility as a model for living. Following Paul's teaching here, Christ was an equal with God, but he did not insist on keeping this equality. He freely surrendered his divine authority, and he took on the form of a servant in order to come into the world as a man. The one who was equal with God became man.

How did Christ show humility? Through his obedience in living in the form of a man, even unto death upon the cross. He could have demanded the obedience of others, yet it was he who was the obedient one. From the height of his divinity, he came low to accept a criminal's death.

What resulted from this obedience, this humility? "God has highly exalted him and bestowed on him the name which is above every name" (Philippians 2:9).

We may ask what this passage teaches us. First, we are urged to have the mind of Christ or humility. Second, humility is to be in the form of obedience to God with Christ as our model for living.

To have the mind of Christ means we are so filled with his spirit that in every situation we almost immediately know the Christian response. We are so accustomed to living in his presence that his mind directs our minds. In the Gospels, when Jesus was asked a question, he never replied that he would have to think about it and give his questioner an answer tomorrow. No, he lived so completely with his heavenly Father that he always responded according to God's will.

In the account about the two young men saving the life of the boy, no mention was made of any discussion of whether they should jump into the water at the risk of their own lives. They did not stop to discuss whether they might themselves drown. Instinctively, when they saw a fellow human being in danger, they tried to save him.

We should profit from the example of Christ and the two brave young men. When another person is in need, if we have the mind of Christ, we will rush to meet that need. Do you have the mind of Christ?

Let us pray:

Lead us, O Father, to so live with the mind of Christ that we shall always follow your will. May we know the path of peace, truth, and right as we seek to be obedient servants. Through Jesus Christ our Lord. Amen.

JANUARY 27, 1980

READ FROM YOUR BIBLE: MATTHEW 16:13-20.

Who Is Jesus?

On Christmas Day, in the year 1642, a three-pound baby was born to Hannah Newton, whose husband had died only a few weeks before. The midwives who attended the mother thought the child would not live until the next day, but, to their surprise, he grew stronger.. His mother named the tiny boy Isaac—Isaac Newton.

Isaac's father had been a farmer, and his mother decided that her son should be one too. He attended school in the village of Grantham, where he boarded with a druggist. The druggist owned books, and although Isaac's mother wanted him to be a farmer when he finished school, young Isaac spent all his spare time reading. His uncle, who was a minister, saw that the boy had a good mind and sent him to Cambridge University. At this famous university, he discovered more books and ideas.

Young Isaac's special interests lay in the direction of mathematics and physics. Today no one knows when he first began to develop a theory of gravity, but he was probably in his early twenties. As a boy, he had a sling that he used to throw rocks. What was the force that held the stone in the sling as he whirled it above his head?

At that time, he had trouble understanding the laws of gravity, so he turned to studying the skies. He made a small telescope, only an inch in diameter and six inches long, yet it could magnify forty times. Soon he was asked to teach mathematics at Cambridge.

Isaac Newton could think his way through the most difficult problems faster than the ordinary person could follow, faster even than he could write. His mind was as swift as lightening. It was almost as if he received his answers by revelation, rather than thought. When he was only thirty years old, he discovered the laws that explain why each planet in the solar system has an orbit and what keeps the planets moving through the skies.

In the scripture reading we have heard today, we learn that Jesus and his disciples were at Caesarea Philippi, far to the north of the Sea of Galilee, near the border with Syria. Up until this time, Jesus had been teaching for the most part about the coming of the Kingdom of God. Now he begins to tell his disciples of his future suffering and death.

In this conversation, Jesus, calling himself the son of man, asks his disciples what people are saying about him. They reply that some say he is John the Baptist (who had been killed earlier by Herod), others say he is Elijah, Jeremiah, or one of the prophets. Then Jesus asks them for THEIR answer. Peter becomes the spokesman for the group and says, "You are the Christ, the Son of the living God."

We should pay careful attention to the reply Jesus made

59

to Peter's statement. "For flesh and blood has not revealed this to you, but my Father who is in heaven." That is, no human being had revealed this fact to Peter. The revelation had come directly from God.

The question Jesus asked Peter is one that comes to every person who considers the claims of the Christian faith. Where does the answer come from? Undoubtedly, the teaching of the New Testament is one basis for our answer. But in our own lives, God himself is a witness to the truth of Jesus' claim that he is the Christ, the son of the living God. Isaac Newton discovered the answers to difficult problems by the use of his mind. We too must use our minds, but we must be open to the direct revelation of God.

The church itself rests on the conviction spoken by Peter on that day. The community of faith rests directly on the fact that Christ is the son of the living God. Does your faith rest on that rock?

Let us pray:

Lord, in the strength of grace, we pray that we may be open to a direct revelation from you on the identity of Christ. Strengthen us when we seem weak, and assure us always of your presence. In the name of Christ. Amen.

FEBRUARY 3, 1980

READ FROM YOUR BIBLE: PSALM 42:1-8.

A Time for Staying Still

The American Indians of northern New Mexico have an unusual custom. Beginning with the tenth of December each year is a forty-day period known as the "Time for Staying Still." These native Americans believe that this is the time for the death and rebirth of Mother Earth. Mother Earth is also known as "Changing Woman," for the Indians have seen the earth young in the springtime, growing to maturity in the summer, mellowing in the fall, and, in winter, sleeping under the snow. Mother Earth is storing up strength for her rebirth in the springtime.

According to the legends of the Indians, the earth cannot be disturbed during this time. Since she is sleeping, one must walk softly. No one can dig in the earth, chop wood, or ride in a vehicle with wheels, for these actions would disturb the sleeping earth. All Indians move into their winter homes during this time when snow usually blankets the land. The blanket of snow symbolizes the blanket of quiet that is a part of this Indian ceremony. On January 20, the "Time for Staying Still" ends.

Another custom these people of northern New Mexico have is the way they instruct their young people in Indian history and folklore. Each winter, boys who have reached the age of twelve or so are taken into a secret underground chamber. For six weeks, they are taught the religious beliefs and customs of their tribe. When the boys and their adult guide finish their six weeks together, the young people as well as their leader have been changed by their experiences because of what has happened to them while they were drawn apart.

The psalm we have heard today is about a person who feels deeply saddened. The writer is living far away from the temple at Jerusalem. He remembers former times when he "went with the throng, and led them in procession to the house of God (verse 4). He says that his "soul thirsts for God" (verse 2).

How often do we "thirst for God"? In the busy world of 1980, many things clamor for our attention. From our rising up in the morning to our lying down at night, there may be many divisions of our concerns. Like many persons around us, we may not devote enough time each day to nourish our spirits.

Spiritual nourishment is of as much importance to a balanced life as physical nourishment. We need food, exercise, and rest for our bodies. We also need spiritual food, spiritual exercise, and spiritual rest.

Maybe the Indians of northern New Mexico have something to teach us with their "Time for Staying Still." Many of us could profit from a time of drawing apart regularly, to study the scriptures, to meditate, and to reflect on God's way with us in the world. Should each of us think about a personal "time for staying still"?

Let us pray:

O Spirit of the living God, descend upon us and fill us with love and joy. Help us to find those times when we may draw apart and feel your presence with us. Through Jesus Christ our Lord. Amen.

FEBRUARY 10, 1980
READ FROM YOUR BIBLE: PSALM 40:1-8.

Making Our Steps Secure

Some of you have seen Mel Tillis, the country music star, on television. Even if you don't recognize his name, you may remember him because he stutters a lot. For many people, stuttering is a handicap, but Mel Tillis has turned it into an asset. He is sometimes on the "Tonight Show," and he is a favorite of audiences because he just plays himself. He can laugh at himself and people respond to him, not out of ridicule, but because he seems to be such a warm and friendly human being.

Like many other people in the world of entertainment, his early life was not easy. Because he stuttered, he could not keep a job. He tried picking strawberries; he worked as a house painter; and for a time he was a railroad fireman. One day after he had lost his job, he applied at a company owned by a man who stuttered. The owner turned him down because there were no openings, but gave him a piece of paper that had on it the words of the old prayer: "God, grant me the courage to change the things I can, the serenity to accept the things I cannot change, and the wisdom to know the difference."

When he read the first word of that prayer, "God," he realized how far he had come from the religion of his childhood. When he was a boy, he had attended a Baptist church. He had discovered that while he was singing he didn't stutter. He loved to sing, and he had dreams of growing up to be an entertainer; but he knew he could not see his dream fulfilled unless he could overcome the problem of speaking. He had asked God to free him from his handicap so he could talk easily like other people. He prayed that he would wake up some morning and his stuttering would be gone. When his prayer was not answered, he gave up his faith in God.

The prayer the man gave him reawakened his sleeping faith. He kept saying the prayer to himself. He resolved to accept the part about serenity in the face of what he could not change, and the wisdom to know the difference.

He kept up his interest in music and began writing songs. He went to Nashville to try for a start in country music. Through Minnie Pearl, he got a chance to play as a backup musician. Then, ten years ago, in 1970, Mel Tillis was invited to play on Glen Campbell's network program. Glen Campbell saw that, even though Mel did stutter, he could be witty and entertaining. From the beginning, people loved him.

Today this well-known man still remembers the prayer he received so many years ago. He could not change his stuttering, but he was able to find serenity through God's help. In time, the very thing he wanted to lose helped him become an entertainer admired by millions of people. This prayer for serenity helped make his steps secure.

The psalm we have heard today contains the words of one who praises God because he has been delivered. He had waited for God; God had heard his cry and had lifted him out of a "desolate pit" and had set his feet "upon a rock" making his steps secure.

The writer continues to praise God for all his wondrous deeds. God desires in return not sacrifice and offerings but open ears. We are to be open to his word to us.

What is the message of this psalm to the Christian of our time? First, we should be open to review our own experience, to see where God has been with us and heard our prayers, even though we did not sense his presence at the time. Mel Tillis did this when he reflected on the gift of prayer. What he had wanted was a job. Instead he got a piece of paper. But the prayer on that piece of paper changed his life. If he had gotten the job instead of the prayer, he might have never become a famous entertainer.

Second, the psalmist urges us to trust in God. "Blessed is the man who makes the Lord his trust." How hard it is sometimes for us to trust in God. So often when we pray, we tell God what is best, and then ask him to make it happen. When we pray in this way, we are a long way from Jesus, who prayed that God's will might be done, even if it meant his death on the cross.

Third, this psalm tells us what God wants from us. He does not want sacrifice and offerings, but delight in doing his will. When we live by this faith in the Lord, we will find that God makes our steps secure.

Let us pray:

Fairest Lord Jesus, give us faith that will not shrink even when our prayers are not answered according to our own will. Lead us to come to you day by day and to live so closely in your presence that your will becomes ours. Through Jesus Christ our Lord. Amen.

READ FROM YOUR BIBLE: EPHESIANS 4:25-32.

The New Life of Love

In the scripture passage we have heard, Paul appeals to the Ephesians to put away their evil ways and adopt the new life of love. Evil talk may soon lead to evil actions.

The names Bonnie and Clyde are part of American folklore of the 1930s. In a movie made a few years ago about their lives of crime, they were pictured as two likable young people whose pursuit of thrills led finally to their deaths. This movie version is far from the truth. In fact, Bonnie and Clyde were mean, vicious killers.

Bonnie Parker and Clyde Barrow met in a Dallas cafe in January 1930. Clyde had already begun a life of crime, and Bonnie was a bored young woman looking for excitement. After Clyde was picked up by police and had been sentenced to two years in jail for earlier crimes, Bonnie smuggled a pistol to him in the Waco jail, and he escaped. He was caught again and sent to prison. In February 1932, he was released from prison and he vowed that he would die before he came back. He did.

During 1932, 1933, and 1934, Bonnie and Clyde committed crime after crime. Unlike other gangs of the time, they did not go after big money. Instead, they robbed small stores, cafes, and filling stations. Often they killed just for the thrill of it.

In July 1933, they barely escaped when police closed in on them in Iowa. For the next ten months, they were on the run. A Texas ranger followed them for more than three months, trying to find the right time and place to capture them. On May 23, 1934, near Gibland, Louisiana, Bonnie and Clyde drove into a police ambush and both were killed instantly. With their short careers of crime and violence, they had given the devil many opportunities.

In the passage we have heard today, we are urged to be watchful lest evil enter our lives when we are off guard.

Earlier in this chapter from the letter to the Ephesians, Paul warns the people about the Gentiles, his term for pagans. Their understanding is darkened, he says, and they are alienated from God because of their ignorance and hardness of heart. The Ephesians are urged to put off their old nature that belonged to their former lives and to put on their new nature, "created after the likeness of God" (Ephesians 4:24). This nature leads to the new life of love.

How do we prove that we have a new nature? Paul offers some specific examples. We should speak the truth with our neighbors; we should never let our anger go beyond the end of a day. We should do honest work so that we can give to those who are in need. We must not engage in evil talk. Finally, he says, "Let all bitterness and wrath and anger and clamor and slander be put away from you, with all malice, and be kind to one another, tenderhearted, forgiving one another, as God in Christ forgave you" (4:31-32).

The basic message of this passage is that all Christians must put on the nature of Christ. Is this a once-and-for-all decision? Not for most of us. Most Christians are engaged in a lifelong school of Christ. Our commitment to put on and to keep the nature of Christ must be made anew every day. We may be tempted to think that we can relax our guard, but, when we do so, we give the devil the opportunity to tempt us to return to our old nature. It is the grace of God coming to us through the power of the Holy Spirit that enables us to hold to the nature of Christ. The old hymn, "Amazing Grace," speaks for us in these verses.

> Through many dangers, toils, and snares,
>   I have already come;
> 'Tis grace hath brought me safe thus far,
>   And grace will lead me home.

Let us pray:

Almighty and everlasting Father, we pray that we may take on and keep the nature of Christ, living the life of love, and that we will demonstrate it through restraint in anger, speaking the truth with our neighbors, putting away all malice, and being kind, tenderhearted, and forgiving. We pray in the name of Christ. Amen.

READ FROM YOUR BIBLE: ISAIAH 35:5-10.

The Day of Everlasting Joy

Since New Testament times, there have been many Christians who are more concerned about the "last days" of the world than the present. These Christians have often speculated on the signs of those last days, though Jesus said that even he did not know the day or the hour when the end would come. Only the Father knows that (Mark 13:32).

However, despite these words of Jesus, many Christians have tried to prophesy when the last days will fall upon the world. Some of these so-called prophets have claimed to be Christ himself and others have claimed to be the prophet or king who has been sent by God to prepare the way or the return of Christ.

In a town in northwestern Europe there came such a man. His name was John. He claimed to have direct revelations from God, and many simple people believed him. He declared that God had directed him to abolish the town council and set up a new government with himself as the head. The people believed him, and he had laws passed that were unusually severe. For instance, the death penalty was begun for all those who disputed authority—a child contradicting a parent, a wife her husband, or anyone who spoke out against the government. Anyone who married a person who was not a Christian could be tried and executed.

Soon, even this much authority was not enough for John, the man who called himself a divine prophet. One day he proclaimed that God had sent him a message that he was to be made king of the whole world. Again the people believed him.

Though he also claimed to be the Messiah of the Last Days, he began to act like an earthly king. He gave new names to the streets of the town and to the days of the week. New-born children were even named by the king.

John himself began to act in ways that made people wonder. For instance, he had several wives, most of them under twenty years of age. He wore fine robes and expensive rings. People who complained were put to death. When an army surrounded the town, he claimed he could work miracles, such as turning stones into bread. In time, the town was captured, and the man who had claimed to be the Messiah of the Last Days was himself killed.

The passage of scripture we have heard today is a symbolic description of the days when the Jews will be returned to their land after a time of suffering. The Jews were saddened because of their misfortunes. Isaiah, the prophet who wrote this passage, is telling them that God will come and save them. Those who have suffered physical illness will be healed, and there will be "streams in the desert."

Christians will associate the pictures in this passage with Christ's promises of everlasting life. Many people come to a time in life when they are worried to the point that they long to be relieved of the burden of earthly existence. They think about God's promises in the Scriptures, and they want to taste that life where there is no sorrow, no suffering, no pain, no tears. They think of the day when they will inherit these promises as a day of everlasting joy.

In this passage, we are also reminded of God's judgment. Those that are unclean will not walk in God's Holy Way. As part of our thoughts of the future, we should remember our obligation of purity before God. Since we cannot by our own power live a life of complete purity, we must confess our sins before God and ask for his forgiveness and mercy in the name of Christ. Let this be our life's goal as we long for that day of everlasting joy.

Let us pray:

God of love and power, give us purity of heart. May our lives belong to you, to whom we give final loyalty. In the spirit of Christ we pray. Amen.

MARCH 2, 1980

READ FROM YOUR BIBLE: EZEKIEL 36:26-32.

A New Heart

In December of 1967, the attention of the whole world was drawn to South Africa, where medical history was being made. On December 3 of that year, the first successful heart transplant took place. The heart of a young woman killed in an automobile accident was given to a man who was slowly dying of heart disease. He only lived about two weeks.

The second transplant took place early in January of 1968 in the same hospital in Cape Town, South Africa. A dentist by the name of Philip Blaiberg had had several heart attacks in previous years, and his condition was getting worse. He had had to give up his dental practice, and by September, 1967, he was so weak that he spent most of his time in bed.

By December, his doctors told his wife to expect the worst at any time. Although his first heart transplant failed early in December, Blaiberg was selected to have another one. He was admitted to the hospital to be ready when the next heart became available. On New Year's Day in 1968, a young man had a stroke on a beach only twenty miles from Cape Town. The man's wife and his mother consented to allow his heart to be used to replace the ailing heart of the dentist.

Early the next morning, after the young man had died, a medical team removed his heart and the transplant operation was begun. It was completed after several hours,

69

and the heart-lung machine was turned off. This was the critical moment. But when the machine stopped, the transplanted heart began beating.

Soon transplant operations were being tried in the United States. Many were successful, and the patients lived for a time, some longer than others. The dentist in South Africa enjoyed several months of improved health. But early the next year, 1969, he was still having problems. On August 17, 1969, he died also. He had lived with another man's heart for nineteen months and fifteen days.

Medical science still has not overcome the problems connected with the transplant of a human heart. Perhaps in the future, operations of this kind can be performed to give years of added life to those whose hearts are failing.

The portion we have heard today from the book of Ezekiel is a prophetic word to the people of Israel. There are four main divisions to the book of Ezekiel. The first division is a prophecy of judgment against Judah and Jerusalem because of idolatry. The second section of the book is a series of chapters condemning the foreign neighbors of Israel. The third section predicts that Israel will be restored, and the fourth division is a vision of the restored community. The passage we have heard today is from the third section, which says that God will give his people a new heart and a new spirit.

Why did the people need a new heart and a new spirit? According to the prophecies of Ezekiel, as well as the other great prophets of the Old Testament, God's judgment had fallen upon Israel because of their rebellion against him. They had begun to worship other gods, and they became military allies with heathen nations. They no longer trusted God, even though he had appealed to them. Because they were stubborn and would not listen, he would not spare or pity them. The people of Jerusalem were worthless, Ezekiel said in chapter fifteen, and were like a faithless wife.

But then the prophet becomes more hopeful and writes of the restoration of the nation. He speaks of God as the good shepherd. God will make a covenant of peace with the

70

Jews. In the vision of the valley of dry bones, Ezekiel speaks of the people being gathered again.

The essence of this part of the prophet's message is that God himself will give the people a new heart and a new spirit. Having a new heart, they will walk according to God's will and become a faithful people.

The heart that was transplanted in the dentist failed, but the new heart given by God will persist. The person with the new heart from God will be clean and will abide by God's law. Let us pray that God will give us a new heart and a new spirit.

Let us pray:

O God of light, we thank you for the promise we have in the Scriptures that you will give us a new heart and a new spirit. Our hearts long for justice and healing and for unity with you, through Christ our Lord. Amen.

READ FROM YOUR BIBLE: JOHN 15:1-11.

Christ—The True Vine

During the first year of the second World War, German submarines damaged and sank many American troop ships. Some United States officials doubted that enough soldiers could be sent to Europe to engage in land war because of the submarines.

In the late summer of 1942, Howard Hughes, the millionaire, was persuaded that an airplane as big as an ocean liner could be built to take American troops to Europe. Hughes was an aircraft designer and builder who at that time held the record for flight from Los Angeles to New York. He sold his idea to officials in Washington, and they agreed to pay him eighteen million dollars to build three big planes.

Aluminum was scarce, and the only plentiful material was wood. So Hughes decided to build the huge airplane out of wood. Because it was to be built of plywood, the airplane had many nicknames, such as the "flying lumberyard."

Hughes had first thought he could build the new plane in about a year, but he discovered that he could not finish it. Work continued year after year. The war ended, and still Hughes had not finished the plane. In 1947, five years after work on it began, the huge plane was ready for its first tests. It was the biggest airplane of its time, over two hundred feet in length with a wingspan wider than the length of a football field.

On a November day in 1947, Hughes invited government officials, military officers, businessmen, and newspaper reporters to Long Beach, California, to watch the tests. Hughes had said that if the plane would not fly he would leave the country and never return. The big flying boat was towed out into the harbor. The engines were started. Slowly the huge aircraft moved across the harbor with Hughes at the controls. On the third run, the plane got up to one hundred miles per hour and took to the air. Hughes flew it about a mile at an altitude of only seventy feet. On that day, he was a national hero.

The fact is that the big plane, also known as the "Spruce Goose," never was reproduced. Up until his death on April 5, 1976, he kept the airplane in a hangar, saying that someday it would be a success. It cost millions of dollars, yet in the end it was worthless. Hughes might as well have destroyed it in 1947, for it never achieved its purpose.

In the lesson we have heard today from the Gospel of John, Jesus says that he is the true vine and his father is the vinedresser or gardener. Every branch that doesn't bear fruit is taken away. As he continues, he tells his disciples that he is the vine, and they are the branches. Those who abide in him will bear fruit. Those who do not will be cut off, thrown into the fire, and burned. In other words, if they do not fulfill the function for which they were created, they will be destroyed.

In the church of every age, including our own, there have been some Christians who do not abide in Christ. At an earlier time in their lives, they may have been close to him. As the years have passed by, they have continued to fulfill the outward obligations of a Christian, such as attending worship and being a part of the organizations of the church. But they have not cultivated the devotional life, the inner life of the spirit, that is nurtured by reading the Bible and engaging in thoughtful meditation about God and his will for their individual lives. As a result, they have lost the inward power and conviction that motivates us to those countless deeds of charity that are at the heart of the Christian life. They have become only the shell of discipleship.

Jesus knew that only those who remained close to him every day could be faithful disciples. If we are to be true followers, we must be as close to Christ as branches are to a vine. We must live in his presence as a part of our everyday existence.

Let us not be like the big airplane Howard Hughes built. It appeared to be the answer to a dream, but the purpose of an airplane is to fly, and it didn't fly—except once. The purpose of the Christian life is to live a life of complete devotion to God and to humanity. Let us remain near Christ, the true vine.

Let us pray:

Heavenly Father, you are the shepherd of all your scattered sheep. Create in us, we pray, a yearning for your spirit. May we live lives of perfect devotion to you as branches of the vine who is Jesus Christ, our Lord. Amen.

READ FROM YOUR BIBLE: JOHN 15:18-27.

Living with Hatred

In the year 1868, one man saved a president.

As the end of the Civil War neared in 1865, President Lincoln developed a plan for bringing the country back together again. He intended to be lenient with those southern states that wanted to return to the Union. Even before his death on Good Friday, 1865, only five days after Generals Lee and Grant had signed the agreement at Appomatox to end the war, Lincoln had clashed with the radicals in Congress. These radicals wanted harsh treatment of the South for several years to teach them a lesson.

After Lincoln was assassinated, Vice President Andrew Johnson from Tennessee became president. Johnson was determined to carry out Lincoln's policy of goodwill. The radicals then tried to get him out of office. In the political heat of the day, the House of Representatives voted to have President Johnson impeached and tried by the Senate on eleven articles.

President Johnson's impeachment hearings began in the Senate on March 13, 1868. Thirty-six votes would be required to put the president out of office. The radical senators were sure of thirty-five votes. The one senator they needed to convince was Edmund G. Ross of Kansas. Ross was threatened in many ways—by individuals in Washington, by the newspapers, and by telegrams from Kansas and other states. He was warned that a vote to acquit the president would mean political death to him.

On May 16, 1868, the vote was taken. One by one the names of the senators were called. Finally, the chief justice, who presided at the trial, came to Ross's name. Every eye in the senate chamber was on him. As Ross later wrote, "Every fan was folded, not a foot moved, not the rustle of a garment, not a whisper was heard." Then he gave his answer in a voice that could not be misunderstood: "Not guilty." Johnson was not impeached.

Ross's critics were right. He was denounced, called a traitor and a skunk. He was hated everywhere. When his term ended in 1871, he returned to Kansas and edited a newspaper.

Edmund Ross lived for thirty-nine years after his famous vote. But public opinion toward him slowly changed. The hatred of 1868 changed to appreciation. Shortly before he died in 1907, the governor and legislature of Kansas sent him a message of esteem for his conduct during the impeachment trial of President Johnson. He had stood by his convictions, even though it yielded him a lifetime of disappointment because he was so despised. He knew the cost of living with hatred.

As Jesus neared the end of his earthly ministry, he knew he was hated and that his life would be required. He also knew that those who hated him would transfer their hostility to his disciples after his death. So in this passage he is warning his disciples and encouraging them to be strong in their faith.

As history shows, his prophecy was true. For three hundred years after his death, the church was persecuted and faithful Christians suffered terribly for their faith. A few surrendered in the face of threats, but hundreds of thousands were faithful to death.

Does such hatred against Christians exist in our world today? Regretfully, the answer is yes. A minister denounced political corruption in the community where he lived, and his wife got phone calls saying that she and their chilren would be killed unless the crusade was stopped. But the minister was firm in his belief that it was the will of Christ that he persist, so he did not stop. In another community, a businessman took what he believed was a Christian stance on a local matter. Public opinion went against him, and a boycott of his store was begun. Soon he went bankrupt and lost his lifetime savings.

On many local and national issues, the Christian may have to choose between popularity and conscience. The threat is not with death for most of us, as for Jesus and early Christians, but hatred may be expressed in other ways intended to hurt. Friends may stop speaking, and the person may be avoided, sometimes even in church.

But more is at stake than a popularity contest. Like Edmund Ross, who saved President Andrew Johnson, we may suffer in the world. But faithfulness to Christ is our commitment, and if we are faithful, his reward shall be ours.

Let us pray:

God of the past and of the future, lead us to be faithful to our commitment to Christ. With each new day, and through all the coming years, help us to see that your mercies never fail. Through Jesus Christ our Lord. Amen.

MARCH 23, 1980

READ FROM YOUR BIBLE: JOHN 12:27-36.

Walking in Darkness

The entire country and much of the world watched the drama that took place in Kentucky in February 1925. A man was trapped inside a cave and every effort was being made to get him out. The name of the man was Floyd Collins.

Collins had always been fascinated by caves. A few years before, he had discovered a cave that became a tourist attraction. Now, in 1925, he had gone into a sand hole near where he lived to see if it led to a cave. When he had not returned the following day, a neighbor crawled into the sand hole and discovered that Collins was trapped sixty feet below the surface. His leg was caught under a fallen rock.

Soon rescue efforts were started. Three men went down into the cave with food for the stricken man and a harness with which they hoped to free him, but their efforts failed.

76

An asphalt company sent men and equipment to the scene to help in any way they could. A railroad sent a hundred men. A wealthy woman sent two surgeons thinking they might try to amputate Collins' leg at the place where it was caught. The Red Cross sent food, tents, and cots for the rescue workers. Thousands of people came to watch the attempts being made to save Floyd Collins.

Lying in the wet darkness far below the earth's surface, Collins learned of the efforts being made to save him, and he told a reporter to tell the workers that he loved them all. Then the passageway caved in, leaving the trapped man totally alone.

In churches all across the United States prayers were said for the safety of Floyd Collins. The president of the United States, Calvin Coolidge, expressed his hope to reporters that Collins would be saved from his dark, wet prison.

Using picks and shovels, a new shaft was begun from the surface. The work went very slowly. Finally, on February 16, more than two weeks after he had been trapped, the workers reached the level where he lay. A shaft was cut into the passageway, and one of the workers crawled into the cavern. In a moment, he returned and said one word: "Dead."

It was decided to bury Floyd Collins where he lay. The cave was sealed and funeral services were held on a bluff above the sand hole. The death of this Kentucky man had attracted the sympathy of a nation.

In the reading today from the twelfth chapter of the Gospel of John, Jesus spoke for the last time to the crowds. He had less than a week to live before he would be crucified, and in those last days he spoke only to his disciples.

In his last public discourse, Jesus is looking toward the days ahead, toward his own death. Though his soul is troubled, he says he will not ask to be saved from this hour, for this is the purpose for which God had sent him.

Here Jesus again used the image of "light" to speak of himself. On an earlier occasion, the gospel refers to Jesus as "the light of men" (John 1:4). In the Old Testament, the Word of God created light in order that there might be light

77

in the world (Genesis 1:3). As the Christ, Jesus' light shines in the world of darkness to give humanity some sense of direction. In John 8:12, Jesus again speaks of himself as "the light of the world."

In our passage for today, Jesus, knowing his death is near, tells his disciples that he will be with them only a little longer. He says that while he is still in the world to show the way, they should move in the direction he shows them. As they trust in his light, they too shall become sons of light. They will then be able to show others the right way.

Floyd Collins died alone in the darkness. We must ask ourselves today, are we following Jesus Christ, the light of the world? Or are we perishing? Is he for us like a lighthouse on a rocky seacoast that warns us that sin is near? Are we sons and daughters of light that point others in the direction of Christ?

Let us pray:

We ask, O God, that you help us go in the direction of the light of Christ, that we may be united with him. We pray in his name. Amen.

MARCH 30, 1980

READ FROM YOUR BIBLE: JOHN 17:16-26.

Helping the World Believe

The man who invented the telephone, Alexander Graham Bell, was trained as a teacher of deaf-mutes. He was born in Scotland where his father had developed a system of speaking to help correct the problems of persons who stammered or had other speech defects.

Bell moved to Canada in 1870. Before he came, he had had an interest in the telegraph. In his experimental work, he was trying to find a way to send several telegraph messages at the same time over a single wire. For his experiments with the telegraph, he had a transmitter set up on one floor of a building where he was working and a receiver on another. The first experiment worked only to the extent that sounds could be heard, but the listener could not understand what was being said. This much was discovered in June of 1875.

Bell continued to work, using different materials. On March 10, 1876, the inventor spoke to his assistant in another room, saying, "Mr. Watson, come here, I want you." Mr. Watson heard him clearly.

This first use of the telephone was only the beginning. At that time, speech could be transmitted only one way over a short distance. By August of 1876, Bell had succeeded in finding a way to transmit a human voice over several miles. By October of that year, he had developed instruments that enabled two persons to carry on a conversation. Only a month later, by using telegraph company wires, Bell was able to talk to his assistant one hundred miles away. By the following spring, he had had a conversation between New York and Boston.

After these successes, Bell became a celebrity. He demonstrated his new invention to distinguished audiences in a number of American cities and in Europe. He received many honors. Scientific societies in both Europe and America showered him with medals and prizes. Today telephone systems span the nation and the world, and a person in the United States can hear a person halfway across the world as clearly as one across town. The invention of the telephone truly wrought a miracle in communication.

The text we have heard today from the Gospel of John is about another type of communication. The seventeenth chapter is known as "the high priestly prayer" of Jesus. The reason is that in this prayer Jesus offers his life as the perfect sacrifice for the sins of the whole world. He then consecrates his disciples in service to bring the world to God.

The first part of this chapter is Jesus' prayer for himself.

He knows the hour has come. He asks that the gift of eternal life be given to his disciples.

The middle part of the prayer is a prayer of consecration for his disciples. He has taught them, and they have received his teachings in faith.

The third part of the prayer, which we have heard today, is for the whole church of the future. He prayed that all his followers would live in a spirit of unity, of oneness, just as he lives in unity with God. With this spirit of unity his disciples would convince the world that he was sent by God.

We should notice here that Jesus was not speaking of an organization to be called "the church." Instead he was speaking of the invisible church, all those who had in common the fact that they were his disciples.

How well has the church lived in a spirit of unity? The sad fact is that in almost every age since Christ lived on the earth, there has been division in the church. A few times Christians have gone to battle against other Christians. Wars that began in Europe during the time of the Reformation went on for nearly a hundred years.

Does a sense of unity live among Christian people in our time? We hear of factions and divisions within a church. Persons of different views oppose each other. Sometimes the divisions become heated, and Christian charity may be forgotten.

As Alexander Graham Bell invented the telephone by which persons can communicate, let us also discover ways to communicate the love of Christ. In his prayer, Jesus prayed that all may be one. Let us work to be the instruments of communicating the oneness we share in Jesus Christ.

Let us pray:

Holy God, we praise your name as we bow before you. Give us insight and support our fainting spirits. Help us to find ways of communicating the love of Christ, in whose name we pray. Amen.

The Miracle of Transformation

In January, 1956, five young missionaries were killed by jungle Indians in South America. The men had been working with the Indians, and they thought they had become friends. They were not, of course, the first missionaries that had been killed by people they were trying to win to the Christian faith, but what happened after that was unusual.

Two of the widows of the slain missionaries, Betty Elliott and Rachel Saint, decided to remain in South America in the hope of returning to work among the people who had killed their husbands. They based their decision on what they believed to be God's will. They faced the obstacles before them with determination.

The biggest problem was how they could ever be accepted by the jungle Indians. They prayed and waited for an answer. In the meantime, they studied the language. Their prayers seemed to be answered when two Indian women came out of the jungle. They stayed for several months, and the widows became friends with them. The American women also made great progress in learning to speak the language.

When they felt they could speak well enough to work among the Indians, they and the two Indian women moved back to live with the tribe that had killed their husbands. Living in the same type of huts as the Indians and eating the same food, they began to talk to the people about God and his son, Jesus Christ. They preached and prayed with these jungle people, giving special attention to the children.

A *Life* magazine photographer and reporter interviewed them in the jungle and asked them why they had decided to go back to that particular tribe. They both said that it was not because they wanted to carry on the work their husbands had begun. The reason they gave was simple. After a great deal of thought and prayer, they were convinced that going back was the will of God.

Here was a case where grief and sadness were transformed into a mission of love.

The passage we have heard from Paul's letter to the church at Corinth expresses the Christian's confidence in life after death. In every age, people have longed for immortality. Among Greeks and Egyptians, there was a wistful hope for immortality but no evidence. The gods of the Greeks were believed to be immortal, but there was no assurance for the ordinary individual.

This longing for eternal life became a possibility after the resurrection of Jesus. Paul picks up a theme he had introduced earlier in this long chapter on the resurrection. In our test for today, he talks about the change that will come about for the Christian. Though we have physical bodies and are therefore perishable, we shall be changed so that we receive a spiritual body that is imperishable. As Paul says here, "This mortal nature must put on immortality" (I Corinthians 15:53).

Immortality has therefore become a reality for Christians. For ancient peoples, this hope was vain. Although they longed for assurance that death was not the end, they did not find it. The resurrection of Jesus Christ made it real.

What effect should this belief have on our lives? First, we should give thanks to God for the gift he has offered us. Second, we should take account of the way we express our thanks. The widows of the missionaries who were killed sought to express their thanks by devoted service to the people who had murdered their husbands. They were led to this step, they said, because they were seeking the will of God. The Christian who wants to express thanks to God will find ways to express that gratitude through service.

The change brought through Christ is truly a miracle of transformation.

Let us pray:

Our heavenly Father, we thank you for the promises we have in the scriptures that give us a sound hope for life after death. Help us find ways to express this gratitude through service to others. In the name of Christ. Amen.

APRIL 13, 1980

READ FROM YOUR BIBLE: GALATIANS 3:23-29.

Neither Jew nor Greek

The 1800s were years in which hundreds of thousands of foreign people came to America. To people in the countries of the Old World, the United States was a place of promise. Those who came to America often wrote to family members and friends who stayed behind, urging them to join them in this wonderful land of opportunity. America was described as a utopia for the common man.

The farm laborer in Germany learned that a day's wages in his homeland would buy an acre of land in the United States. If he rented farm land, he discovered that for half the amount of his yearly rent he could buy a farm twice as large as the one he rented. If he already owned land, he could sell it, pay the cost of bringing his family to America, and still have enough left over to buy four times as much land as he owned in the old country.

When immigrants came to America, they tended to settle near others from the same country. For example, Germans settled in cities such as St. Louis, Cincinnati, and Milwaukee. There they had German-language newspapers, a library, bands and orchestras, German theater, and churches where their native language was used.

A crisis occurred that tended to change immigrants into Americans. That crisis was the Civil War. While the older immigrant stayed on his farm, his son marched away to war with the village company of volunteers.

Two things happened. First, the older immigrant who did not fight became concerned about the war. His attention was drawn away from the old country and concentrated on his new homeland. After all, he had a son who was fighting for America. Second, the son was thrown with other young men of his own age. In the heat of battle, he saw his comrades not as German or Irish but as American.

When some of the boys came home, they were heroes—American heroes. Those who fell in battle were buried in far-off cemeteries—but it was American soil. Thereafter, the newcomers thought of themselves as Americans.

In the text we have heard today, Paul was writing to the Galatians about the law and the gospel. Under the Jewish law, Christians could learn about their obligation toward God, but they did not have the *power* to enable them to live out a life in harmony with that law. To use a modern illustration, they were like a railroad locomotive without fuel. Though the goals of the law were clear, like the locomotive, they could not move toward perfection.

With Christ came the gospel. The gospel provided the power through the Holy Spirit, as well as the way. Through Christ, Paul wrote, they became children of God. As God's children, all other distinctions were thrown away. It no longer mattered whether you were Jew or Greek, slave or free, male or female.

This teaching is instructive because we tend to make too many distinctions between nations, status, and gender. When citizens of one country think they are better than citizens of another country—when one group in society becomes convinced that they are better than other groups—when males think they are better than females, or vice versa—pride has entered the heart, and because pride separates us it is foreign to our unity in Christ.

Paul tells us that we are one in Christ. When we begin to feel that our church is superior to another church, that our group is more righteous than another, we are violating that unity. The obligation to see ourselves united in Christ does not mean that we must all be alike or act alike, but it requires that we see others as God's children also, even when we think their ideas and views are wrong.

The crisis of the Civil War provided a sense of unity among immigrants who had moved to America. The crisis that provided Christians with a sense of unity was God's decision to send his son into the world. The law is no longer the center of religion; instead, we have become children of God through faith.

Let us pray:

Lord, we believe that the gospel of your son brings both the way and the power to lead us to you. Forgive us when we sow disunity in the church for reasons of pride. Help us to be instruments of unity among all your people. In the name of Christ. Amen.

APRIL 20, 1980

READ FROM YOU BIBLE: JUDE 17-25.

Convincing Some, Saving Some

Most of northern Europe was converted to the Christian faith through the word of a missionary by the name of Boniface. This missionary was born in England and converted when he was very young. Early in his life, he decided that he wanted to commit all his days to God. His first missionary work was among the people of what is today Holland. Next he moved into the area that later became Germany.

At that time the Germans believed in spirits of pagan gods. These gods were thought to live in fire, water, storms, the sun, and the moon. Certain springs and trees were believed to be sacred. The people built temples dedicated to their gods, where they had ceremonies at certain times of the year.

85

Although Christianity had spread into those lands earlier, it was still weak. The people had had little training in their faith, and they sometimes mixed elements of their old religion with belief in Christ. The pagan cults were still strong.

Wherever Boniface went as a missionary, he tried to win pagans to the religion of Jesus. Since the people believed in magic, sometimes that belief was involved in their conversion. Once Boniface went into an area where the Germans worshiped under a sacred oak tree. He decided to cut down the tree in order to show the people that it was not sacred. The pagans that were watching cursed him while he cut the tree, but before he had finished, a powerful gust of wind blew the tree down. They were so impressed that they gave up their old gods, became Christians, and built a chapel out of the lumber from the sacred oak.

Boniface worked for more than forty years among the Germans. He was able to win many leaders to the Christian faith, and they in turn helped convert the masses of people. He and his helpers did odd jobs with their hands to support themselves because the people were too poor to pay them. In each community where he worked, he built a log building before he left, and one of his disciples remained behind as the leader of a band of new Christians.

Like most missionaries, Boniface was confronted with many dangers. As an old man, he set up a camp near a river. A group of drunk pagans attacked the camp, and Boniface was killed.

Working among nonbelievers, he won many of them because he was a man of prayer who was also courageous, kind, and steeped in the Scriptures. For half a century, he lived among foreign people. Often he felt a sense of failure because paganism remained so strong, but he never gave up. He knew that God was with him.

The short letter of Jude, from which our reading today has been taken, was written at a time when the Christian faith was in crisis. Ungodly persons were trying to corrupt "the faith which was once for all delivered to the saints" (verse 3). Jude condemns these people and warns his fellow Christians against their deeds of ungodliness. He describes them as "grumblers, malcontents, following their own passions, loud-mouthed boasters, flattering people to gain advantage" (verse 16). They are scoffers "who set up divisions, worldly people, devoid of the Spirit" (verse 19).

Then Jude gives some positive instructions to those who would be faithful to Christ. They should build themselves up in the "most holy faith," keeping themselves in the love of God, waiting for "the mercy of our Lord Jesus Christ unto eternal life." They should try to convince those who doubt and save some of those who are facing God's punishment.

These words from Jude apply to all Christians today. Among those who claim to be following Christ there are some in our time who are following their own ungodly ways. Some are grumblers and malcontents. Some boast. Some flatter people to gain advantage over others. Some set up divisions. Some are worldly people, devoid of the spirit.

If we are trying to follow Christ, we are to first of all pay attention to our own lives. We should make every effort to build up our faith and keep ourselves in the love of God. Jude urges us not to judge or condemn others. In verse 9, he points out that when the archangel Michael was contending with the devil, Michael did not pronounce judgment over the evil one. Judgment belongs to God. Our role is to try to convince those who doubt and to save others from the Lord's punishment.

Boniface, as missionary to the Germans, lived in danger of his life for more than fifty years in order to take the gospel to pagan people. We do not need to go among pagan people in foreign lands to be faithful to the gospel. Our mission field can be right here in our own community, where we may witness by convincing some and saving some from God's punishment.

Let us pray:

Lord, help us not to become people like those Jude knew, claiming to follow Christ but in fact ungodly, grumbling malcontents, worldly, and devoid of the Spirit. May we witness here in our community, convincing some to follow you. In the name of Christ. Amen.

APRIL 27, 1980

READ FROM YOUR BIBLE: PSALM 43.

Against the Ungodly

Elijah Lovejoy loved peace, but he was a man willing to back up his convictions with his life. He taught school in his early years, but he felt the call of God and became a minister. After studying at Princeton, he moved to St. Louis in 1833 to edit a church paper. In the 1830s, the people of the United States were becoming divided over slavery, and Elijah Lovejoy began to preach and write about this problem. Many of his readers protested, so he decided to move from St. Louis.

In 1836, he settled in Alton, Illinois, where he took a job as editor of a newspaper that opposed slavery. The people of the town did not like his views, but he continued to express his convictions. When a printing press for his newspaper arrived by boat on a Sunday, Lovejoy refused to unload it because he would not work on the Lord's day. That night, his enemies dumped it in the river. Another press was ordered, and, after it arrived, the editor continued to express his views on freeing the slaves. Soon the second press was destroyed by his opposition.

The people of the town asked Lovejoy to leave, but he felt God had called him to work for abolition, so he refused. A third press arrived, and it was unloaded and placed in a warehouse at night by the editor and his friends. At a meeting of the townspeople, he made a moving speech in which he declared that he had the right to speak and write about his ideas. This right, he said, was given to him by God and guaranteed by the United States Constitution. He said he could not be silent, even though his life was threatened, because he feared God more than he feared the mob.

As he and several friends were guarding the warehouse where the press was stored on the night of November 7, 1837, a mob came to set fire to the building. As Lovejoy came out of the warehouse to urge the mob not to burn down the building, shots rang out and the editor was hit by five bullets. He was able to get back to the door before he fell and died.

In a speech shortly before he died, Elijah Lovejoy said that almost every hand in town was against him. At a town meeting he asked for any person he had injured or molested to stand up and speak against him. No one stood up. He told the people that soon the crisis would be over, and they would say, "He was right, he was right." Although he had violated no laws, he said he was pursued through the streets like a criminal. But the officers of the law would not protect him.

After Lovejoy's death at the hands of a mob, his cause was won by others. Slavery was abolished, and people lived to say, "He was right, he was right." But the ungodly had snuffed out his life.

In Psalm 43, the writer asks God to defend his cause against an ungodly people. He begs for the light and truth of God in order that he might be led by them. Looking within himself, he asks why he is cast down when his hope is in God.

If we look back on the life of Elijah Lovejoy, we cannot say whether we would have followed his course if we had been living in those times. But we can learn from him of a faith and life totally committed to God. How would we feel if we were trying to follow God's will, and every hand in the community was raised against us?

Lovejoy was convinced that God was with him. As much as he wanted others to like him, he could not submit to the mob. Why? Because, as he said, he feared God more than men. He was never charged with any crime, but he was executed at night by a cowardly mob.

Christians today need the kind of faith Elijah Lovejoy

had. He believed he was following the example of Jesus Christ. If Jesus had quietly left Jerusalem during the week before his crucifixion, he might have lived to be an old man. But he was convinced that he was following God's will, and this led to his death on the cross.

Like the psalmist, we should pray for defense against ungodly people. In God, we shall find our refuge, our hope, and our help.

Let us pray:

Eternal Father, we pray that we may earnestly seek your will in all that we do. Once we know it, we ask for the courage to stand by it, no matter what opposition we face. Through Jesus Christ our savior. Amen.

MAY 4, 1980

READ FROM YOUR BIBLE: I JOHN 3:11-18.

Seeing a Brother in Need

Arthur Tappan made a substantial fortune as a businessman in New York. Instead of using the money he made on personal luxuries, he gave his wealth freely to help others who were in need. When he was starting out in business as a young man, he reflected seriously on his responsibility as a steward of God.

Arthur Tappan was born into a family that took religious obligations seriously. His parents were strict about the observance of Sunday. There was no Sunday school in the town where they lived, so the children were given training in Christian education at home.

When Arthur was fifteen years of age, he became a clerk in a hardware and drygoods store. By the time he was twenty-one years old, he had established his own business.

90

He soon began to prosper through the use of what was then a novelty—he sold his goods for cash only and to everyone at the same price. Most merchants charged the highest price they could get from each buyer, but Arthur Tappan charged everyone the same price.

As his wealth grew, he continued to think about his stewardship. He was a heavy contributor and an officer in many religious organizations, such as the American Sunday School Union, the American Bible Society, and the American Home Missionary Society. He gave heavily to educational institutions and paid the educational expenses of many young men studying for the ministry.

He was a builder of churches and a supporter of the revival movements of his time. He and his brother built the Broadway Tabernacle in New York as a place for Charles G. Finney, the most popular preacher of the day, to speak to thousands of people each week.

Because he was a champion of some unpopular movements, he was violently criticized. His business suffered, and he was threatened personally with abduction, assault, and assassination. He listened calmly to all the abuse heaped upon him and ignored the threats. He deeply believed that he was on God's side of the issues, and that he should work to bring God's will to earth. When he saw a person or group in need, he would do whatever he could to help, no matter what it cost him.

In our reading today from the third chapter of First John, we are reminded again "that we should love one another." And what is the test of love? John answers that question with another question: "If any one has the world's goods and sees his brother in need, yet closes his heart against him, how does God's love abide in him?" His fellow Christians are then admonished "not to love in word or speech but in deed and in truth."

The counsel of First John is wise for us today. As Christian people, we may not confront great need face to face. When we do not, our love is often expressed only in words or speech. But such expressions are not enough. If we are to follow the admonition of our text, we must open our hearts to those in need, expressing our love in deed and in truth. Arthur Tappan was that kind of Christian. Are we?

Let us pray:

Heavenly Father, forgive us when we are blind to those in need around us. Make us sensitive to those who are lonely and discouraged. May we express our concern, not only in word and speech, but also in deed and in truth. Through Jesus Christ our Lord. Amen.

MAY 11, 1980

READ FROM YOUR BIBLE: REVELATION 3:1-6.

A Dying Church

About one o'clock on the afternoon of August 24, A.D. 79, the city of Pompeii, a few miles south of Naples, Italy, was slumbering in the summer sun. It stood a short distance from Mount Vesuvius. Seventeen years before, an earthquake had taken place, but it had been forgotten. Shortly after one o'clock, the commander of the Roman navy, who was with his fleet in the harbor a few miles away, saw a cloud of smoke above Mount Vesuvius, which had once been an active volcano.

By morning the next day, the sky was darkened with the ashes and smoke that poured forth from the mountain. The volcano had become active again. Earthquakes jolted the entire area.

When the mountain first exploded, the people of Pompeii were terrified. Panic swept the town. Many families sought safety in inside rooms or cellars of their homes. As the lava and ash continued to fall, some hoped to escape by leaving home. Scores of people were killed in the streets by stones falling from crumbling buildings.

For four days, the deadly rain of lava and ashes fell on the city. During those days, the sun was blacked out because of the fragments of carbon spewed into the air by the volcano. On the morning of the fourth day, the sun was again visible, and where Pompeii had stood there was silence. The entire town was buried under twelve feet of stone and ash. People who had lived in the city were cast like statues when masses of lava poured over them. Slaves in chains died in their barracks. A woman was found sitting at her dressing table among her jewels. The master of the house and his wife and children were found in an underground passage of their home.

Some of those who escaped returned and tried to dig for their possessions. The lava and ash were so deep that they soon gave up. After a while, Pompeii was again silent, a dead city.

John, the writer of the book of Revelation, had a vision of the church at Sardis. He is told by the heavenly Christ to address to the guardian angel of that church some words that are very critical of it. Although the church at Sardis has the appearance of being alive it is dead. Its works are far from perfect. Its members should keep in mind what they have heard and repent of their sins.

Not all the people of Sardis are guilty. Their garments are clean and they will walk with Christ because their lives are worthy. All those who conquer over sin and remain faithful will not have their names blotted out of the book of life. This is an absolute guarantee of eternal life. The heavenly Christ will confess that this person is faithful before God and the angels.

The idea of the book of life grew up among Jewish people in the period before the birth of Jesus. The Jews believed there was a book of life in heaven where the names of the righteous were written. Some Jews also believed in a book of destruction as well. If a person's name was written in the book of life and he later turned to sin and evil, that

93

individual's name could be removed and written in the book of destruction.

This passage of scripture teaches us the importance of being awake and alive to the gospel of Christ, not asleep or dead. If we have been Christians for many years, it is easy for us to grow lax or weary toward our privileges and obligations. We may come to the place where our faith is a formal religion in which we do only what we must, finding little joy in Christian service.

When we grow cold in our commitment to Christ, we are like petrified trees or the dead city of Pompeii. What was living has been turned to stone.

We must remain awake and pure in the hope that we can be counted worthy and can walk with Christ. If we conquer temptation and sin, we will inherit the promise of the heavenly Christ that our names shall not be blotted out of the book of life.

Let us pray:

O God, we ask you to help us so that we will not be like the church at Sardis, having only the appearance of life. May our names be written in the book of life and may we daily walk with Christ. In whose name we pray. Amen.

MAY 18, 1980

READ FROM YOUR BIBLE: PSALM 24.

At the Gates of the Temple

During the Middle Ages, the castle was the home and fortress of a lord. In those days, warfare was almost constant, and military protection was important. As people began to settle in villages, the settlements often grew up around a castle.

Many castles were built at the top of steep hills, so that the enemy had to get up the hill before an attack on the castle could begin. As they climbed the hill, the attackers would be at a disadvantage, because the defenders could use arrows and heavy stones that would roll down and crush the attackers.

Around many castles built on level ground was a deep ditch called a moat. This ditch was often filled with water. A drawbridge lay across the moat in peacetime, but when the castle was under attack, it could be pulled up. When an enemy attacked a castle that had a moat around it, they had to cross the water before they could try to climb the walls.

Around the top of a castle wall ran a ledge called a rampart. Here the defenders stood as they threw spears and rocks and shot arrows at the attackers.

The lord and his family lived in the most protected part of the castle. This area was called the keep. Servants lived on the lower floors, and the lord on the upper floors. The keep could be easily defended even if the rest of the castle was captured or destroyed.

The major purpose of the castle was to shelter those who lived inside from attack. Its design was intended to keep the enemy outside. Even in times of peace, the peasants who farmed the lands around the castle, and the people who lived and worked in the village were not welcomed. Its gates were shut except to the few the lord invited to come in.

How different was the temple, the holy place in Jerusalem, to the Hebrews. Each year, in a special ceremony, the ark of the covenant was carried through the streets of Jerusalem to celebrate the fact that God was the king. At the end of the procession, the ark was carried by the priests up the hill of Zion where the temple stood. The priests asked the people two questions: "Who shall ascend (go up) the hill of the Lord? And who shall stand in the holy place?" The question was then answered: Persons who are clean in both their outer and inner lives, or, as the psalmist states, "he who has pure hands and a clean heart, who does not lift up his soul to what is false." He must be honest and "not swear deceitfully." Persons who have these traits will be blessed by the Lord and are worthy to come up the holy hill and enter the temple.

The temple was the most sacred place in the Jewish faith. All were welcome to approach it, but only the righteous were expected to enter. The temple was exactly the opposite of the castle, whose design was intended to keep people out.

In the psalm we have heard, the procession stopped before the temple gates to ask the doors to open in order that the ark, which symbolized the presence of God, might come in.

By this ancient ceremony in Jerusalem, we are reminded of our own attitude toward worship. Is our church more like the temple—or the castle? Do we welcome all who come or are there some who want others to stay out? When we come to worship, do we come with clean hands and a pure heart?

Let us pray:

Our Father in heaven, we pray that our fellowship may be open to all your children. May we have the pure hands and clean hearts that you expect of all those who follow you. In Jesus' name. Amen.

MAY 25, 1980

READ FROM YOUR BIBLE: ISAIAH 65:17-25.

A Hope for a New Age

Twenty years ago, public concern in the United States over a nuclear war was high. The Joint Congressional Committee on Atomic Energy held hearings from time to time to learn from scientists what might happen if the country were attacked.

Scientists said that a ten megaton bomb would make a hole in the earth two hundred forty feet deep and nearly half a mile wide. It would destroy every brick home or apartment house within seven miles. Frame houses as far away as ten miles would be flattened, and window curtains up to twenty-five miles away would catch on fire from he heat of the blast. As electric lines, gas mains, and fuel storage tanks were destroyed, many fires would start. About twenty minutes after the blast, a fire storm would begin. This fire storm would consist of winds blowing toward the burning city at a velocity of thirty to forty miles per hour. More people would be killed during this fire storm than would be killed in the blast itself.

Scientists estimated that as many as two hundred sixty-three hydrogen bombs might fall on the United States in one day during an all-out attack. Fifty-four million people would be dead or dying. Twenty-one million buildings would be wrecked. Within seven hours of the attack, a third of the nation would be covered by the fallout, and in another two days nearly half the nation would be. Not only would crops in the fields be ruined, but also vast areas of farmland could not be used for many years since it would be contaminated.

There would be millions of defective births over the next thousand years, and some genetic damage could be expected as far as ten thousand years from the time of the attack. The meaning of that statement is that within a few generations nearly every American would be defective.

These horrible possibilities will continue as long as nations use physical power to settle their disputes. In the tense days of the Cold War during the 1950s and 60s, the prospect of nuclear war seemed great. Because many nations now are capable of making atomic and hydrogen bombs, the danger is still with us. As the threat becomes greater, nations have seemed more willing to use reason to settle disagreements, but world tensions sometimes threaten to explode.

Today we have heard a passage from the book of Isaiah. The second half of that book (chapters 40–66) deals with three major themes: the coming of the Lord (40–48), the redemption of Israel (49–55), and warnings and promises

(56–66). The portion we have heard today is one of the promises.

Isaiah, like many of the prophets, always looked for the hand of God in human affairs. He saw the old age passing away and the new age beginning. The end of the present age would mark a new creation. Christian leaders also looked toward a new age. In Isaiah 65:17, God says, " 'For behold, I create new heavens and a new earth.' " In the vision of John found in Revelation 21:1, the writer also speaks of seeing a new heaven and a new earth.

Christians today have lost faith in God's willingness and power to come into human history. We hope that the leaders of nuclear nations will not begin a war; but we fail to see that God can prevent war, using human leaders as his instruments. We sometimes see God as a small god, too weak or uninterested in coming to the assistance of his sons and daughters.

The view—that horses or chariots or nuclear submarines or hydrogen bombs—will achieve a final victory is soundly condemned by the major prophets. They all agreed that trust in God was more important in the long run than weapons.

Isaiah has a vision of a new creation that would be a time of peace and joy. As Christians, let us trust in God, and let us work and pray that God's will for peace on earth may come to pass. This is the hope for our new age.

Let us pray:

Lord of all space and time, we earnestly pray that the world will never be destroyed by bombs made with human hands. May the leaders of the world see your will and find ways to establish enduring peace in our world. In the name of Christ. Amen.

READ FROM YOUR BIBLE: JEREMIAH 16:10-15.

Worse than Our Fathers

When the Pilgrims landed at Plymouth in the year 1620, they got help from friendly Indians. In that first cruel winter, nearly half the new settlers died. The Indians looked on them as helpless children, and they showed the Pilgrims how to plant corn and to catch fish. For many years, the Englishmen and their Indian neighbors lived in peace.

As more settlers came to America, they began to take Indian land and push the natives West. For nearly two hundred years, white men killed the Indians who fought for their land. The Indians lacked the military power of the white man, and the tribes did not always have leaders who could unite them. In 1829, Andrew Jackson became president of the United States. In his first message to Congress, he said that all Indians should be moved west of the Mississippi River. Jackson, who was called Sharp Knife by the Indians, knew that white settlers and the natives would never live together in peace.

Congress passed the law Jackson recommended, and the first Americans were given extensive lands west of the river. No white person would be allowed to live there. The Indians would be safe from further aggression.

Before this law could be put into effect, new settlers moved west of the river into Indian lands. In 1848, gold was discovered in California, and many people who were originally on their way out there stopped and settled in the lands promised to the Indians. The west coast was colonized, and Kansas and Nebraska were admitted as states.

Many chiefs thought they could negotiate with the white men, but treaty after treaty was broken. In the end, Indian tribes lost their native lands and were forced to give up their way of life. The kindness that Indians had shown the Pilgrims in 1620 was only to be repaid by later settlers who took their lands and killed the natives who fought for them.

The Pilgrims were good to the Indians, but the whites who came after them were worse than their fathers.

According to the prophet Jeremiah, the Hebrews would be taken off to Babylon and would live in captivity. In the passage we have heard today, the people ask why has the Lord pronounced against us? "What is our iniquity? What is the sin we have committed against the Lord our God?" The Lord also gave Jeremiah the answer. The prophet was to tell them that their fathers had gone after other gods and had served and worshiped them. They had forsaken the Lord and had not kept his law.

But furthermore, Jeremiah went on to tell the people that they had been even *worse than their fathers*. They had followed their own stubborn will and had refused to listen to him. For that reason, the Lord would send them to a strange land and would show them no favor.

In our nation today, largely as a result of the television program "Roots," more people than ever are trying to find out something about their ancestors. They visit libraries, courthouses, cemeteries, and churches to try to learn something about the people who came before them. We tend to hope for something sacred and worthy of honor among all those who are a part of our family tree. We can still honor our ancestors, but at the same time recognize that they were not perfect. After all, they were human too.

Each generation should try to understand both the strong and weak points of those who have lived before. We should become wiser and stronger because of the past.

As Americans, we need to look at our history. In light of our broken promises to the Indians, we can try to learn something from the past. We hope that God will not judge us as being worse than those who lived before us.

Let us pray:

Almighty and everlasting God, the aid of all who call upon you, we pray that we might learn from the past and be wiser and stronger. Forgive us when we commit the sins of past generations and refuse to learn. Through Jesus Christ our Lord. Amen.

Saints in the Land

The Red Cross is the world's best-known agency for disaster relief. It was started in Europe partly because of the work of Florence Nightingale on the battlefields of the Crimean War. In 1863, a conference met in Geneva, Switzerland, and formed that organization. Its work was first with the sick and wounded in times of war.

The AMERICAN Red Cross grew out of the work of Clara Barton. During the Civil War, Miss Barton was working as a government employee in Washington. She was also a volunteer worker among the wounded of the war and became known as the "angel of mercy." She went to Europe and there learned of the Red Cross. When she returned home, she was determined to found a Red Cross society in the United States.

From the time of its organization, the American Red Cross developed a program for disaster relief. Under Miss Barton's leadership, its aim was to provide help for average citizens who could not help themselves. With the assistance of trained volunteers, the Red Cross started a rural health nursing program. Later, lifesaving and water safety programs were organized.

During the first World War, local chapters of the Red Cross rolled bandages and set up canteens for soldiers both at home and overseas. Ambulances and hospitals on the battlefields were staffed by the Red Cross, and most soldiers returned from that war with sincere appreciation for the work of the organization.

In 1926, a hurricane in Florida was followed by a flooding of the Mississippi River. In both these disasters, the resources of the organization were called on as never before. Since it was established, the American Red Cross has assisted in more than six thousand relief operations.

One significant aspect of the work of the Red Cross is the

fact that it enlists so many volunteers. It is supported by
contributions from interested people, and its work is done
largely by men and women who give their time. These
volunteers are like the "saints in the land" that we have read
about in today's passage.

This psalm is a psalm of trust. The writer is setting forth
his faith that fellowship with God provides the highest
satisfaction. It begins with a profession of his dependence
upon God. " 'Thou art my Lord; I have no good apart from
thee.' " He wants to remain always in God's presence, for
there he finds strength and happiness.

He says that he finds delight in associating with the saints
in the land. In company with others who are like-minded, he
finds his own life enriched. He and they have chosen God as
their portion. God give him counsel, even in the night. He
keeps the Lord before him, and thus he cannot be tempted
or moved away from the will of God.

The psalm we have heard today is an account of one
individual's relationship with God. Our attention is directed
to the second verse. "As for the saints in the land, they are
noble, in whom is all my delight." We should be careful not
to neglect the role of fellowship in building up our Christian
lives.

Among the Jews, there was a belief that a synagogue could
not be established unless there were ten men and that no
service of worship or study could begin until a group of ten
were present. Although solitary prayer is worthy, the
Hebrews put great emphasis on the fellowship of the saints.
As we associate with other persons of faith, our own faith is
built up. We also help to build up the faith of others.

In fellowship with the saints of God, we are like burning
coals in the grate of a fireplace. Each coal nourishes the
others. But if one coal drops through the grate to the hearth
below and lies there alone, its heat will gradually grow dim
and its fire go out.

Finally, we should note that the word saint does not mean
a perfect person. It is used to apply to any person who is
dedicated to God.

The Red Cross has been able to bring help to hundreds of

thousands of disaster victims because thousands of volunteers have worked together. Christian fellowship is made stronger when we join with the saints in the land—to understand and to do the will of God.

Let us pray:

Almighty God, we express our thanks to you today for all the associations we have in Jesus Christ. May we experience the fellowship of the saints in order that the fires of faith may burn brightly. In the name of Christ. Amen.

JUNE 15, 1980

READ FROM YOUR BIBLE: PSALM 15.

Who Is Holy?

In a certain community there lived a barber. He was popular with the men, and they often stopped in to visit with him, even when they didn't need a haircut. They would discuss sports or hunting or fishing or any other topic that came to mind. Because the barber was active in the church, he would not allow bad language to be used in his shop. If one of his customers had a lengthy illness, the barber would visit him at home or in the hospital to cut his hair. When he left after cutting the sick man's hair, the patient nearly always felt better because the barber was so cheerful. Altogether, the barber was a fine influence for good in his community.

The city elections were coming up, and several of his friends and customers suggested that he run for the city council. At first, he only laughed at the idea, but as others mentioned it, he began to think seriously about it. He could serve the community, and he could certainly use the extra money, because costs were going up and he had little money put aside for his retirement.

He agreed to run, and he was elected easily. After he began to attend the monthly council meetings, he began to see that a great deal went on that he had not known about. For instance, when certain laws were changed, he found an envelope with cash in it under the door of the barber shop the next morning. Someone was merely trying to express appreciation for his vote in the council meeting.

One night, a man appeared before the council hoping to get a zoning law changed. A supermarket chain wanted to lease a large parcel of his land. Some people who lived near the land in question came to the meeting to protest the change in zoning. The vote was postponed for a week.

That same evening, soon after the council adjourned, the man who wanted the zoning changed went to the barber's home. The landowner talked about the profit he could make if the supermarket chain were allowed to build a store on the land he owned, and he even offered to share the profits with the barber. The next morning, when the barber opened his shop, he found an envelope under the door with two thousand dollars in cash in it. He knew where the money had come from.

The next week, the council voted to change the zoning, and the barber voted with the majority. He felt he had earned the money under his door. One of the members of the council who had been on the losing side reported that the landowner had tried to buy his vote.

In a trial held soon after, the popular barber was convicted of accepting a bribe and sentenced to three years in prison. Thus was the reputation of a friendly man destroyed.

A bribe is defined as any gift made with a view to corrupting the behavior of anyone who is in a position of trust. The psalm we have heard today asks who is worthy to worship God on the holy hill where the temple is located.

The writer's answer is the person who

- walks blamelessly
- does what is right

- does not slander with his tongue
- does no evil to his friend
- does not reproach his neighbor
- despises the reprobate
- honors those who fear the Lord
- keeps his word even when it may cause him to be at a disadvantage
- doesn't ask interest on money he loans
- does not take a bribe against the innocent

The person who met these qualifications could approach God in worship. For Christians, this list offers us something to think about as we consider our own worthiness and holiness.

Let us pray:

Our Father in heaven, help us to make our walk blameless before you, to do what is right, and to keep our word. We pray that we may take seriously the obligation to live a godly and holy life. In the name of Christ. Amen.

JUNE 22, 1980

READ FROM YOUR BIBLE: PSALM 20:1-8.

Remembering the Name of God

Edward Gibbon was the great historian of the Roman Empire. He tried to understand why an empire that lasted a thousand years declined and finally disappeared. He found six causes.

First, he said that the Romans lost faith in themselves and their institutions.

Second, the democracy established in early Rome finally gave way to dictatorship. The emperors who came to power were cruel almost beyond imagination. Many were murdered, and a man who killed an emperor replaced him as head of the empire.

Third, Roman citizens lost pride in the empire and were unwilling to serve in the army in defense of the state. Defense was left to barbarians who were hired to serve in the army and were paid in either money or plunder. These barbarians saw the weak spots of the empire they were supposed to be defending.

Fourth, the empire was so large it could not be governed effectively. The decline of Rome in a sense resulted from its greatness.

Fifth, the form of Christianity adopted in Rome's western empire emphasized a passive rather than an active religious life. The virtues of a vigorous Christian faith were not brought to bear on the problems of Roman society.

Sixth, the Romans were not aware of the growth and movement of barbarians outside the empire, and when hordes of them attacked, the Romans were surprised and unprepared to meet them.

Thus did the greatest empire of the ancient world crumble into the dust of history.

The psalm we have heard is a prayer for victory and assurance of God's help. In the church today, we should pray for the victory of the faith. We can also learn how to avoid some troubles in the church if we look at the reasons Rome fell.

First, we should not lose faith in the power of the Christian gospel. Once we begin to doubt the strength of the gospel to deal with personal and social problems, defeat is almost certain.

Second, we must hear the voices of all Christians in the church. The church should not be dominated by one person or a few.

Third, we must be willing to defend the church against its enemies.

Fourth, we must not be misled by the notion that size equals greatness. A small church fellowship can be powerful. A large church must not be overtaken by pride.

Fifth, our faith must be active in dealing with the issues that confront our communities, our nation, and the world. A passive faith that accepts the world's values has little to offer.

Sixth, Christians must be aware of the power of evil forces that are set against the values which the Christian church stands for. The first requirement for victory is to be aware of the opposition.

This psalm is a prayer on behalf of the king. The writer asks God to protect the king and send him help in time of trouble. He prays that God will fulfill all the king's plans. In the second half of the psalm, the writer expresses faith in God's help. Though some boast of chariots and horses, he says, "we boast of the name of the Lord our God." Though the enemy will collapse and fall, "we will rise and stand upright." The final verse is a petition to God: "Answer us when we call."

This psalm serves as a reminder to us that all power comes from God. The Roman Empire fell in on itself because it had no inner strength or vitality. The church or fellowship that lacks these qualities cannot "rise and stand upright." Strength and vitality come out of closeness to the presence of our heavenly Father. If we learn to live in the presence of God, he will answer us in our day of trouble.

Let us pray:

Almighty God, we pray that our fellowship may have the vigor and vitality that comes from a sense of closeness to you. May we avoid all the qualities that make the church weak in times of crisis, and may we add to its strength and power. In the name of Christ. Amen.

READ FROM YOUR BIBLE: PSALM 137:1-6.

By the Waters of Babylon

White spirituals and gospel songs have played a big part in American churches. They are not as well known perhaps as the Negro spirituals, but they played a similar role.

In the early years of the Protestant Reformation, people were taught to sing about their faith. But singing that really came from the heart arose in large part out of the revival movement in the United States.

Early in the nineteenth century the first camp meetings began in Kentucky. They spread over the whole country. Often there were no song books, so the leader would have to teach the group the words as well as the tune. The songs were the kind that had a chorus or refrain that the congregation could learn easily. Sometimes a leader would change a song or add new verses. An illustration of this type song is "On Jordan's Stormy Banks I Stand." The leader would sing the verse:

> On Jordan's stormy banks I stand
> And cast a wishful eye,
> To Canaan's fair and happy land
> Where my possessions lie.

Then the whole congregation would join in on the chorus:

> I am bound for the promised land,
> I'm bound for the promised land,
> Oh, who will come and go with me,
> I am bound for the promised land.

As people moved to the cities following the Civil War, many of these white spirituals were forgotten because the larger churches sang different songs.

Gospel songs arose among city congregations who were

looking for music like that they had known from camp meetings in rural areas. Unlike the white spirituals, which were passed on from one group to another and often changed in the passing, gospel songs were composed by individuals, both their words and music. Ira Sankey, the song leader for Dwight L. Moody, the revivalist, was one of the best known composers.

Both white spirituals and gospel songs came from the heart. They enabled a group to express the joy of their religious faith.

In the psalm we have heard today, the writer speaks about songs and sadness. He and his people were captives in Babylon. They were far from home. They had no spirit for singing. Their captors and tormentors mocked them by asking them to sing some of the songs they had sung in Jerusalem.

This request caused the writer to reflect on memories of the holy city. He would rather lose the use of his right hand and the ability to speak than forget Jerusalem.

This writer helps us to see how important religious faith was to the Hebrews who were far from home. While in Jerusalem, they may have thought very little about their blessings, but when they became captives, what they had lost seemed especially dear.

The sad tone of this psalm over what the people have lost prompts a question in us. Do we take the right to worship as we choose too much for granted? During this coming week, we will be celebrating the birthday of our nation. Along with the holiday, we should thank God for freedom of worship. In many lands in the world today, people do not have this right. Since we have it, we may not think often about it. But should we lose it, we would be like these homesick people by the waters of Babylon.

Let us pray:

We thank you, Lord, for a free land and for the right of freedom of worship. May we never take our freedoms for granted. We pray in Christ's name. Amen.

READ FROM YOUR BIBLE: PSALM 25:1-15.

The Paths of God

In the highlands of Appalachia, near where the states of Kentucky, Tennessee, and Virginia meet, is the Cumberland Gap. The Gap is lower than the surrounding mountains, and for centuries Indians had used it as a pathway. They called it the Warrior's Path. It connected with the vast system of trails used by Indians and buffalo in the southeastern part of the United States.

In the early days of settlement beyond the mountains, men who were called Long Hunters went hunting in Kentucky and Tennessee on expeditions that sometimes lasted a year or more. Daniel Boone was probably the best known of the Long Hunters. Though they were sometimes robbed by Indians, they kept making trips through the Cumberland Gap and improved the trail.

In time a mail route was established through the gap. For many years, the Wilderness Road, as it was called, was little more than a path, not passable for wagons.

As more settlers moved west on the Wilderness Road, efforts were made both by Kentucky and Virginia to improve it. Sections were leased out to contractors who provided the labor and materials. After their section of the road was completed, they had the right to erect gates across it and collect tolls from travelers. Many people did not want to pay, and armed men were required to be certain that the tolls were collected.

For fifty years after Daniel Boone and the Long Hunters blazed the trail, the Wilderness Road was the best way to go through the mountains.

The portion of the twenty-fifth psalm we have heard today is divided into two parts. The first seven verses are a prayer for help. The plea for divine aid is common to many psalms. The writer lifts up his soul before God and professes his trust in the Lord. He begs that he not be put to shame, and that his enemies not find joy in his troubles.

Then he asks God to show him the Lord's ways. This prayer should be on the lips of every Christian. So often in life we come to a crossroads and must make decisions that have far-reaching consequences for ourselves and others. We cannot see clearly all the results in the future. We weigh the choices open to us. Alone, we cannot see which decision would be better. Even when we enlist the assistance of our friends and family, we cannot be certain. We call on godly friends for their counsel, but they too cannot show us a clear way. Do we then call on God in order to know his ways? If we fail to do so, we may make a serious mistake.

The writer goes on to ask God to teach him the Lord's paths. In the early days of the Wilderness road through the Cumberland Gap, there were many forks in the trail. The new traveler had to watch carefully to find the trees that had been notched by Daniel Boone and the Long Hunters. If he missed the trail, he could lose valuable hours before discovering his mistake. One could get lost and perish in the wilderness. But if the the traveler followed the path that had been marked, he would find the way to his destination.

So we too should attend to the paths of God. He will lead us through life if we will call on him. He is a loving father who desires good for his children.

As the psalmist says:

> Good and upright is the Lord;
>   therefore he instructs sinners in the way
> He leads the humble in what is right,
>   and teaches the humble his way.
> All the paths of the Lord are steadfast love
>   and faithfulness,
>   for those who keep his covenant and his testimonies.

Let us pray:

Grant, O Lord, that we may follow your paths all our days and that your ways may become our ways. Teach us humility and help us to keep your covenant and your testimonies. In the name of Christ. Amen.

111

Crying Aloud to God

Twenty-one men stood in the prisoner's dock in the courtroom, all charged with treason. Many had been tortured. All had confessed. The date was March 2, 1938. The place was the city of Moscow in the Soviet Union. All were later shot.

During the years from 1936 to 1940, more than eight million Soviet citizens were arrested and tried for what the government called crimes against the state. If a man was arrested, his wife and his parents might also go to jail only because of their relationship to him.

Many of these arrested were executed. Some never received anything like a fair trial. Those who were not killed were sent to labor camps. Most of these camps were in Siberia. Being sentenced to a camp was almost the same as execution, for prisoners usually did not live long.

After prisoners received sentences, they were taken from the local prison to railroad cars of the type used to haul cattle. The journey would often last several weeks. The cars were not heated, and they were terribly uncomfortable in both winter and summer. There was little food or water, and the guards were brutal.

When the prisoners arrived at the camp, their troubles got worse. They were awakened at five o'clock in the morning, and they were allowed only ten minutes for breakfast, their best meal of the day. Then they were marched off to work in gangs of twenty or thirty. The order was given that the prisoners should not talk or look around while marching. A misstep to either right or left would be considered an attempt at escape, and the escort would open fire without warning. The prisoners worked in mines, in forests, on construction jobs, in the blazing heat of summer and the paralyzing chill of winter. They had five minutes to eat their thin soup at noon. The work continued until darkness came. Then the long walk back to the camp. After five minutes for supper, they went to their barracks. The large rooms where they slept were crowded and uncomfortable. The prisoners slept on boards covered with straw or sawdust.

Millions of Soviet citizens were sent to these camps. Most of them died and were buried in unmarked graves. This was the time of the great purge under Stalin.

These wretched people had no one to call on. Whole families would disappear, never to be heard from again. No protection was available. Each village had its quota of prisoners to fill. Even if no one was guilty of crime, the officials had to arrest the number they had been given, and when the accused were tried, no attorney was available to plead for their rights.

Although communism taught atheism and the churches had been closed, many of the people turned once again to their faith for comfort in that age of terror. But anyone who publicly professed belief in God committed a capital crime and could be executed.

The psalm we have heard today is a cry for help. Both day and night, the writer seeks the Lord in prayer. Yet he feels that God is far away. He believes the Lord has turned away from him, that God's love has ceased, that God is angry with him.

Many Christians today have known times when they have felt far from God. Sometimes his love seems distant and his promises unrealized.

The remainder of this psalm praises God. The psalmist remembers the mighty deeds of the Lord, the wonders that have been shown to all people. As he reflects on these works, he asks the question: "What god is great like our God?"

This psalm instructs us, first of all, that when we feel God has left us alone, we should acknowledge this to God. When we think about our sense of aloneness, we are opening an opportunity for God to speak to us. Second, we should follow the example of this writer. When we feel God has gone away from us, we should think about the mighty deeds and wonders of the past. In that way, we may again sense the presence of God. Unlike the wretches of the Soviet prison camps who were not allowed to worship, we have a heavenly Father. No god is great like our God.

Let us pray:

Master of the world and universe, we acknowledge that we sometimes feel that you are far away. When we have the experience of distance, we pray that we will remember your past deeds in the world. In the name of Christ. Amen.

JULY 20, 1980
READ FROM YOUR BIBLE: LAMENTATIONS 3:21-33.

Great Is Thy Faithfulness

Easter, the Christian holy day, falls at the same time as the Jewish Passover. Mark 14 describes the Last Supper of our Lord as the Passover meal of Jesus and his disciples.

The Passover is the first of three great festivals in the Jewish faith. It originated as a memorial to the Exodus, when God sent the plague of the death of the first-born child in order to get the pharaoh to let the Jews leave Egypt. The Jews were to kill a lamb and put its blood on the doorposts of their homes. If there was blood on the doorposts of the house, the Lord would "pass over" that house, and the first-born child would not die. The twelfth chapter of Exodus commands the Jews to keep the festival every year as a way of remembering that God saved them.

Among religious Jews all over the world today, the Passover is still observed by ritual in the home. The youngest child asks the question: Why is this night different from every other night of the year? In the ceremony that

114

follows, certain foods are eaten that remind the Jews of their history. For instance, a bowl of salt water on the table reminds them of the tears of the people during their slavery in Egypt. Toward the end of the ceremony, the front door of the house is opened to call to memory the night of watching in Egypt more than three thousand years ago. In this way, Jews of every age make the experience of the Exodus their own.

At Easter, we Christians recall the most important events of our faith, the beginning of the Lord's Supper, the crucifixion, and the resurrection of Jesus.

Actually, however, the Passover for Jews and Easter for Christians should be celebrated at all times, not just once each year. In the text we have heard today from the book of Lamentations, we are called to remember the mercies of God. Lamentations is a book of sorrow. It was written after Jerusalem was captured by the Babylonians and the temple destroyed. Although God's judgment is important in this book, hope is also a part. The verses we have heard today lift up that hope.

We are reminded here that the steadfast love of God never stops, his mercies never end; "they are new every morning." His faithfulness is great, and the Lord is part of the faithful soul. The Lord is good to those that wait for him and hear him. One should wait quietly for the salvation of the Lord.

These are words of encouragement for us today. Sometimes we become discouraged and feel that we are far from God. When we have such feelings, we should remember the promises in the book of Lamentations that God's mercies are new every morning.

For Christians, these words have special meaning. God sent his son into the world in order that we might have peace on earth and the hope of everlasting life. Though God acted two thousand years ago to bring his promise to pass, the good news should be new every morning.

God's faithfulness is great. He is good to those who wait for him. He will have compassion on us.

Let us pray:

O God, we remember at this moment that your mercies never stop and that your promises are new every morning. Your faithfulness is great, and you are our portion. We wait for your salvation in the name of Christ. Amen.

JULY 27, 1980

READ FROM YOUR BIBLE: PSALM 27:1-6.

Set High on a Rock

As long as ships have sailed the seas, unseen rocks have caused shipwrecks. From the time before the birth of Christ, towers were built on shore near dangerous rocks to warn ships. Today lighthouses still serve that purpose.

St. Paul Island, in the Atlantic Ocean off the shore of Canada, is a small mass of granite. In the past, ships have sometimes struck rocks off the shore of this island and have sunk. Survivors have tried to get ashore, but many of those who made it were so battered they bled to death on the shore. If there were survivors, they would look for driftwood to light a fire that could be seen on the mainland of Canada, only a few miles away. When fishermen went out to the island each spring, they always found the frozen bodies of wreck survivors who had waited vainly for a rescue that never came.

In spite of the number of lives that were lost, there was no lighthouse on St. Paul Island. Then a tragedy occurred that got public attention. A ship named *Jessie* was driven on the rocks in a snowstorm. Weeks later, when fishermen went to the island, they discovered that twenty-seven people from the ship had gotten ashore. For ten weeks they survived until the food was gone. One by one, they died of starvation. A note was left that described those terrible weeks of waiting.

116

Still no move was made to build a lighthouse, even though the public protested. Then a giant storm struck that threw not one ship but four on St. Paul Island. Two years later, the government built two lighthouses.

Today, in the fitful fog, irregular ocean currents, and rain and snowstorms, the two lighthouses warn the ships at sea of danger. No longer do the rocks of the island present a danger, for upon those rocks stand the lights of warning.

The image of the lighthouse seems fitting with the text we have heard today. The psalm opens with the words:

> The Lord is my light and my salvation;
>   whom shall I fear?
> The Lord is the stronghold of my life,
>   of whom shall I be afraid?

The writer begins by professing his trust in the Lord. He looks to God to be his light, to show him the godly path, and to be his salvation. God is the stronghold of his life, so he has no need to fear. Even if his adversaries and foes are all about him, his heart is not afraid.

He asks only one thing of the Lord, that he may dwell in the temple of the Lord. For it is there that he feels the nearness of God and a sense of divine protection. He is certain that in the day of trouble God will set him upon a rock.

The words of confidence we find in this psalm offer encouragement to us. We are sometimes rebuffed when we are trying to do good. Our motives are misunderstood, and we feel cast down. A special concern may not turn out as we had hoped, and we feel a sense of despair. Those from whom we expected support leave us standing alone. Even those closest to us, family and friends, may not sense the depth of our emotion and the hurt feeling of abandonment.

In such an hour when we need consolation, the words of this psalm can bring us a measure of peace. God is our light and salvation. He can come to us as the lighthouse appears out of the storm to help those who are nearing the rocks of St. Paul.

If God is our stronghold, there is no one to fear. Even if

117

we are surrounded by those who do not support us, we can be confident in God who will hide us in the day of trouble and will set us high on a rock.

Let us pray:

Almighty and everlasting God, in the hour when we need consolation, we pray that we will profess our trust in you, and that you will lead us to salvation. You are the stronghold of our lives, and we shall have no need to fear. Through Jesus Christ our Lord. Amen.

AUGUST 3, 1980

READ FROM YOUR BIBLE: PSALM 98.

The Marvelous Things of God

The people of Israel were often called to remember their past. From the time the Jews left Egypt, their religious leaders saw the hand of God in every part of the nation's life. The major periods of their history until the time of Christ are these:

1. The Exodus.
2. Wandering in the wilderness
3. The conquest of Canaan, the Promised Land
4. The period of the Judges
5. The united kingdom under Saul, David, and Solomon
6. The separate kingdoms of Israel and Judah
7. The fall of Israel
8. The kingdom of Judah (alone)
9. The fall of Jerusalem
10. The Exile
11. Israel under foreign rule

118

In each of these periods of their history, the religious leaders saw God at work. The Exodus from Egypt under the leadership of Moses was possible because of the mighty acts of God. The wandering in the wilderness was God's punishment of the people for worshiping the golden calf. After a new generation had arisen, the land of Canaan was conquered, and the people finally possessed the land God had promised Abraham.

After the Promised Land was settled, the rulers were called judges. During the period of the judges, the people would be faithful to God for a time, but then lapse into the worship of idols. After Samuel, the last of the great judges, Saul became the first king. He was followed by David and David's son, Solomon. After Solomon's death, the kingdom was divided into two parts, Israel or Samaria, and Judah. Under attacks from an enemy, Samaria was captured. The southern kingdom of Judah stood alone for a hundred and thirty-five years. When it too was captured, the period known as the Exile in Babylon began. Jerusalem was burned and the temple was torn down. After about fifty years had passed, some of the Jews returned from Babylon. Jerusalem was rebuilt and a second temple was erected.

In these changing fortunes, the Hebrews saw the work of God. All prosperity came because they were faithful, and all adversity because they fell away from worship of the one true God. Their victories in battle were won because God was with them, and their defeats took place when God left them.

The psalm we have heard today is a song of salvation. It must have been written after some important event in the lives of the people, because it speaks of the marvelous things God has done and of his victory in the sight of the nations. Therefore, the song calls the people to praise God by making a joyful noise.

The Hebrew people lived with the conviction that God was with them in their entire history. They got this view by looking over their past. We can picture what they did by using an example from our own experience. When a person drives a car up a mountain road, he or she is careful about all

119

the curves in the road. The driving requires attention, and the driver may be hardly aware of the scenery. But once the car is at the top of the mountain, the driver can stop and look below to see how all the turns in the road led to the top of the mountain.

Our personal lives can be looked at in the same way. When we look back, we often see a pattern that we had not known was there. God has been active in our personal history in ways we did not see before.

As we reflect on the goodness of God in our lives, let us sing to the Lord a new song, for he has done marvelous things.

Let us pray:

O God, you who have built the church upon the cornerstone of Jesus Christ, we also sing a new song to you, for you have pulled us from slavery to sin and given us life everlasting, a marvelous thing. We pray through Jesus Christ our Lord. Amen.

AUGUST 10, 1980

READ FROM YOUR BIBLE: PSALM 130.

Out of the Depths

Martin Luther is generally recognized as the man who began the Protestant Reformation. Although he built on the foundations of those who preceded him, his distinctive contribution influenced church history in a decisive way.

Martin Luther's parents sent him to college in the hope that he would become a lawyer. When he was returning to school from a visit home, however, he was caught in a frightening thunderstorm, and he made a vow that he would enter the service of the church. He was a remarkable student who in time became a brilliant preacher, writer, and teacher.

In the year 1517, Luther had gone so far in his differences with the Roman Catholic Church that he expressed a desire to debate some of the scholars of the church. As he argued and discussed his views with both friends and foes, he saw that he could never return to the beliefs he had held as a younger man.

Four years after he openly began to work for reformation of the church, he was declared an outlaw. For almost a year, Luther's friends hid him in an isolated castle. During the time he was there, he translated the New Testament into his own language and he continued his writing on theological issues. But all was not well with Luther. He suffered from a period of depression brought on because he was out of touch with his friends and supporters.

In the years that followed, Luther increasingly became the leader of the Reformation. Throughout his life, he continued to go through periods of ill health made even worse by low spirits.

In the year 1523, he wrote the following poem that later became a hymn. It is based on the psalm we have read today.

> Out of the depths I cry to thee;
>   Lord, hear me, I implore thee!
> Bend down thy gracious ear to me;
>   I lay my sins before thee.
> If thou rememberest each misdeed,
>   If each should have its rightful meed,
> Who may abide in thy presence?
>
> And thus my hope is in the Lord,
>   And not in my own merit;
> I rest upon his faithful word
>   To them of contrite spirit.
> That he is merciful and just,
>   Here is my comfort and my trust;
> His help I wait with patience.

We can learn from Luther's experience that even the giants of faith have their moments of low spirits. But as the psalm we have heard reminds us, though we are in deep distress, we can call upon God for relief. We are sinners, but God forgives us when we come to him in sorrow. The writer of the psalm sounds a note of waiting on the Lord as watchmen wait for morning.

Like Luther and the psalmist, our hope is in the Lord. "For with the Lord there is steadfast love" (130:7).

Let us pray:

Eternal Spirit, our hope is in you, not in our own merit. We rest upon your faithful word, and we look to you, out of the depths, as our comfort and our trust. Through Jesus Christ our Lord. Amen.

AUGUST 17, 1980

READ FROM YOUR BIBLE: PSALM 122.

A Prayer for Peace

Thirty-six years ago this week, Allied armies were set for the liberation of Paris. Hitler had said that the city would be left in ruins if General Eisenhower tried to take it, but the Germans collapsed and the commander surrendered. The date Paris was liberated was August 25, 1944.

The Allies had landed in Normandy on D-Day, less than three months before. By the end of August, the armies of the free nations were chasing the Germans across northern France and Belgium. For the next three months, the German armies were slowly pushed back. Eisenhower ordered a new offensive to begin in November. Again the enemy armies were pushed back. In December of 1944, the Germans summoned all their strength to try one more offensive. For several days, they made some progress in what was later called the "Battle of the Bulge." This battle was the greatest single battle in the second World War. In a month, however, the Allies had turned back the Germans.

By March 21, 1945, the Allies were at the Rhine River ready to cross over into Germany. Hitler ordered his armies not to retreat, but the Allies were not to be stopped. By early April, the victorious armies were pushing down the superhighways toward the center of Germany.

In Berlin, Hitler continued to order his armies to attack, but the German military forces were falling apart. By the middle of April, Berlin was under attack. On April 22, Hitler saw that the end of the war was near. In his underground bunker in the city of his earlier triumphs, he committed suicide on April 30. A week later, on May 7, 1945, the Germans formally surrendered. Three months later, on August 14, Japan also surrendered. For the first time since Germany had invaded Poland on September 1, 1939, the world was at peace once more.

Thirty-five years have passed since Americans celebrated V-E and V-J days. Peace is still not secure. The threat of war seems always near somewhere in the world.

The psalm we have heard today is a prayer for the peace of Jerusalem. This holy city had known wars and threats of war for centuries. The writer must have been a visitor to the city of Jerusalem from some distance away. He speaks of the joy he felt when he had the opportunity to go up to the house of the Lord. Before he leaves, he offers a prayer of peace.

In our world today, we do not know deep peace. Sometimes even in the church we do not have peace. Like this psalmist, however, we ought to pray for peace. The people of the Old Testament believed that God held all the nations under his control and that peace would come when the nations looked to God.

In the fourscore years of this century, we have seen nations fight in the name of keeping peace. Many organizations have been established to work for peace, such as the League of Nations and the United Nations.

As Christians who believe in the power of prayer, we

should pray for peace in the world as this psalmist prayed for peace in Jerusalem.

Let us pray:

O God our Father, we too look for that sense of joy that comes when we are in your house. We too are glad when we say, "Let us go to the house of the Lord." We pray today for a world at peace, through Jesus Christ our Lord. Amen.

AUGUST 24, 1980

READ FROM YOUR BIBLE: PSALM 91:1-6.

My Refuge and My Fortress

John Knox, who led the Protestant Reformation in Scotland, knew what it was to suffer for his faith. Knox and several others who were opposed to the Catholic Church captured St. Andrews Castle. After they had been there for fifteen months, the castle was captured by the French. Knox and several other prisoners were then forced to serve as galley slaves on French ships.

Life on these galley ships was harsh for prisoners. When the wind died and sails could not be used, the prisoners had to propel the ship with oars. Each oar was forty to fifty feet in length and passed through a hole on the side of the ship. Six men rowed each oar. These men were chained to a bench where they sat and slept.

Sometimes they would have to row as many as twenty hours at a stretch. They were driven by fear of the whip on their bare backs.

John Knox was a galley slave. Although he was in good health at the time he was captured, he got sick. The first year was usually the hardest for the slaves. At the time he got sick,

124

the ship was off the coast of Scotland, his homeland. One of his companions, who knew how ill he was and who thought he was going to die, asked him to turn his eyes toward the land and see if he could recognize it. Knox saw the steeple of the church at St. Andrews, where he had been preaching when he was captured, and said, "God will not let me die before I can preach and glorify his name in that same place."

To the surprise of his shipmates, he did not die. He was finally freed from service as a galley slave, and, within a few years, his hope was fulfilled. He again proclaimed the glory of God from the pulpit of St. Andrews church.

The psalm we have heard today is a promise of security. Living in the presence of God is like living in a refuge or fortress. God protects his people from FEAR of terror, pestilence, and destruction. The distinction the writer makes is an important one. God delivers us from *fear*. If we trust in him and live in his presence, we will no longer be afraid.

During the two years John Knox was chained to his bench as a galley slave, he was underfed, sick, and mistreated—but he never gave up. Even during the time of his physical misery, he knew God was with him.

Fear is a terrible emotion, even though it may have useful purposes. For instance, fear is what keeps a mature adult from picking up a poisonous snake or driving a hundred miles an hour on a wet highway. By the absence of fear, we can often tell the difference between a mature and an immature adult.

But fear can also be a crippling problem. In a situation of fear, danger seems great. A person will have a faster heart beat and tremors. Judgment and behavior become uncertain and untrustworthy. An individual under the stress of fear may perform actions that increase his or her problems. The final stage of fear is panic, when one loses control of behavior. In panic, for instance, when a fire is discovered in a theater, an individual may become paralyzed and unable to move to safety.

The psalm we have heard today promises us that trust in God will remove all fear. Neither the terror of night, nor the arrow that flies at noonday will cause him to be afraid. God makes the same promise to us today.

Let us pray:

O God, who art the father of us all, we have known fear and sometimes panic in our lives. We pray that we may have the certainty of the person who wrote this psalm that you are always with us and will relieve us of fear if we call upon you. In the name of Christ. Amen.

AUGUST 31, 1980

READ FROM YOUR BIBLE: PSALM 51:6-12.

In the Secret Heart

Today public libraries all across the land provide their communities with reading materials that, if purchased by an individual, would be available only to the very rich. We accept the public library as an institution that has always been a part of community life. But this view is incorrect.

The Puritans of New England insisted on the right of every child to an education at public expense. Even this principle was disputed for a long time, but the public school did become a part of the American scene. When the first libraries were built in the United States, they were not free. Everyone who wanted to use a private library had to pay an annual membership fee.

When the idea was proposed for free public libraries, many of its critics called it socialism. If books were to be furnished free to the masses, why not free food and clothing as well?

The man who did the most for public libraries in the United States was Andrew Carnegie. Carnegie was born in

Scotland. When his father had to sell his business, they moved to the United States. Andrew went to work at age of thirteen for only $1.20 per week. He was eventually involved in many business interests, but he is best known for the fortune he made in the steel business.

At sixty-one years of age, Carnegie retired and devoted the remainder of his life to giving his money away. He remembered how scarce books were when he was young, and he designed a plan for making free books available to ordinary people. He offered to give money for a library building to any community that would agree to provide the books and staff to operate it. During his lifetime, he provided the funds for nearly seventeen hundred library buildings.

Critics of Carnegie said that his only interest was in having monuments to his name in towns and cities all across America, but in fact, Mr. Carnegie did not require that his name appear on the library building. His satisfaction came from knowing that the buildings he gave money for would provide free books on loan to millions of Americans. He wanted no credit for gifts that totalled more than forty million dollars.

Carnegie believed that wealthy men should leave only a moderate amount of their fortune to their families and should spend the rest for the welfare and happiness of the common people. They should be trustees concerned only for the good of the community and never giving a thought to personal glory.

How different this spirit is from those who always want credit for everything they do—and sometimes credit for the deeds of other people. The psalm we have heard today asks God for the gift of wisdom in the secret heart. This wisdom would not be for the purpose of bringing glory to the one who received wisdom. Instead it would provide a guiding light to show others the true path to greatness.

Humility is sometimes a lost art among Christians. Arrogance and pride seem more in style. How inconsistent these qualities are with the life of Jesus. His only concern was for others. Can we imagine a Jesus who was arrogant and proud, who boasted of his achievements, who put down others because they were not as great as he?

From a study of the New Testament, we get the opposite opinion of him. As the letter to the Philippians teaches us, though he was in the form of God, he took on human form and humbled himself, becoming "obedient unto death, even death upon the cross" (Philippians 2:8).

Our goal should be to seek wisdom in the secret heart, asking God to wash us and make us clean, filling us with joy and gladness.

Let us pray:

Almighty and everlasting God, we ask you for wisdom in our secret hearts, not for the purpose of bringing glory to ourselves, but in order that we might glorify you. Give us also a spirit of humility, that we might always be willing to share the credit with others of the good things that happen. In the spirit of Christ. Amen.